Praise for *The Alie.*

"It is a difficult path to report news from the tangled web of government denial policies about non-human interactions with this planet. But ultimately, the official phony denials can't last forever in the face of so many firsthand human experiences and testimonies since the historic 1961 Betty and Barney Hill encounter with non-humans in New Hampshire that left physical residues of dress stains, scuffed shoe tops, and an odd pattern of shiny circles on top of their car's trunk. Betty's niece, Kathleen Marden, and her coauthor Denise Stoner, now add from their alien abduction files more meticulously investigated high strangeness with non-human entities in the lives of two American families that have been physically, mentally, and spiritually affected, as so many thousands of other families have been for more than 50 years. Each new voice adds pressure to the question: When will Earth life be publicly introduced to other cosmic life?"

—Linda Moulton Howe, Emmy Award–winning
journalist, author, reporter, and editor of Earthfiles.com

"As a writer and researcher of the unknown, I have always been intrigued by the alien abduction phenomenon. From abduction cases to missing time, Stoner and Marden have brought this mystery to the forefront. Through their personal experiences and in-depth research, this book compels the reader to consider some rather bizarre possibilities. *The Alien Abduction Files* certainly demands a place on my reference shelf—but more than that, it's a book that is long overdue."

—Charlie Carlson, associate producer and host,
PBS Television's *Weird Florida*

"I have known Kathy Marden for several years, lecturing at conferences together, co-presenting on expert abduction panels, and responding to questions from anxious audiences. She is a highly respected colleague for her work, her experience, and her knowledge. The two major cases she presents in her book are compelling, unnerving, and would be unbelievable were it not for her investigation tenacity in searching for 'proof,' [which] has enabled her to provide solid answers in the alien abduction files."

—Yvonne Smith, C.Ht., president, CERO International,
author of *Chosen: Recollections of UFO Abductions
Through Hypnotherapy*

The Alien
Abduction Files

The Alien Abduction Files

• • • • • • • • • • • • •

The Most Startling Cases of Human-Alien Contact Ever Reported

By Kathleen Marden
and Denise Stoner

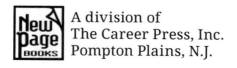
A division of
The Career Press, Inc.
Pompton Plains, N.J.

THE ALIEN ABDUCTION FILES
Cover design by Wes Youssi
Printed in the U.S.A.

To order this title, please call toll-free 1-800-CAREER-1 (NJ and Canada: 201-848-0310) to order using VISA or MasterCard, or for further information on books from Career Press.

The Career Press, Inc.
220 West Parkway, Unit 12
Pompton Plains, NJ 07444
www.careerpress.com
www.newpagebooks.com

Library of Congress Cataloging-in-Publication Data
CIP Data Available Upon Request.

To the courageous abduction experiencers who have stepped out of shadows to tell their stories, and to those who find it impossible to do so.

Acknowledgments

The authors would like to express our gratitude to the many individuals who so graciously contributed to this book and to the 75 participants in the Marden-Stoner Commonalities Among Abduction Experiencers Study. Without their assistance, this book wouldn't have been possible.

Contents

Foreword

There have been a number of supposed sociological phenomena whose reality has been strongly resisted when first proposed. The notion that priests would sexually abuse choir boys and others seemed outlandish, but it turned out to be all too true. The notion that parents might occasionally physically abuse their children was also resisted by the medical community, but now we have laws requiring teachers to report suspected incidents of abuse. The notion that Germany could be systematically murdering millions of Jews, Romani, and others seemed absurd. After all, Germany was a well-educated, highly cultured country, the land of Goethe and Beethoven. U.S. Supreme Court Justice Felix Frankfurter has been quoted as saying about such claims: "I know that what you have to say is true, but I don't believe it."

Abductions of Earthlings by aliens have been reported since the Betty and Barney Hill case was described in *The Interrupted Journey* by John Fuller in 1966, with many more reports since. But many people, especially scientists who can't imagine that such abductions could take place without them knowing about it, have vigorously fought the idea. One problem is that an aura of ridicule has surrounded these phenomena as reported by various journalists and debunkers. Yes, *The UFO Incident* on NBC-TV in 1975 (starring James Earl Jones and Estelle Parsons as Barney and Betty Hill) helped some come to understand the possibility. Still, many can't even seriously consider the notion of alien visitation. Claims have been made that travel between stars is impossible; it would take too much time and energy. Similar foolish claims were made about space flight, travel to the moon, and, before that, even travel in aircraft. Perhaps the epitome of resistance was reached in 2012, when the British Astronomer Royal, Dr. Martin Rees, garnered wide publicity by falsely claiming that "only kooks see UFOs" and that aliens wouldn't come this long way "just to meet with a few cranks." As might be expected, he gave no indication of being familiar with any of the literature by astronomers or psychiatrists such as Dr. Benjamin Simon, who worked with the Hills, as reported in a much later book, *Captured! The Betty and Barney Hill Experience*. Most of the work on the book was done by my coauthor, Kathleen Marden, who is also the coauthor of this book.

This book is, among other things, a well-documented overview of two cases, both involving multiple witnesses and each extending over a long period of time. Denise Stoner and her husband have decided to finally go public with their story, despite some misgivings about the public's reaction. Jennie, whose story is told by Kathleen, has still not been publicly identified. A very important addition to the UFO abduction literature is the data (provided here for the first time in any book) concerning the results of the detailed survey "The UFO Abduction Experiencer" conducted recently by Marden and Stoner.

Marden and Stoner show that abductees seem to share a number of characteristics and experiences not generally shared by non-abductees, who were also questioned as a kind of control group. Furthermore, they have taken the courageous step of discussing the possibility that the reported experiences are the result of something other than alien intervention, such as astral projection, poltergeist intervention, sleep paralysis, and other explanations put forth by the UFO debunking community. They certainly seem to have made the case for alien intervention. It is certainly to be hoped that this book will encourage many more experiencers to come forth to share their experiences. There is also a real need for more involvement by social scientists in investigations of the topic. There have been a dozen PhD theses done on UFO-related subjects. Surely, there is room for many more serious investigations, which means professors (and abductees) being willing to stand up and be counted. The past history of strong, but eventually unsuccessful, resistance to new ideas by academics as reported, for example, in the book *Science Was Wrong* by Marden and myself, has demonstrated that it takes persistence on the part of proponents in dealing with the objections of the debunkers to new ideas and concepts. A great Nobel Prize–winning German physicist, Max Planck, once said that new ideas come to be accepted, not because their opponents come to believe in them, but because their opponents die and a new generation grows accustomed to them. I can only hope the acceptance of alien abductions as real will come sooner rather than later. It has only become obvious quite recently that mankind and Earth are not in the center of the universe or at the top of the heap. The Kepler space satellite has shown there are literally billions of other planets in the Milky Way, not just the nine of our solar system. Work on nuclear fusion, the process producing the energy in all the stars, can provide trips to the stars for us. Now we need to stop spending a trillion dollars a year on military toys. We need to know who the abductors are and why they are kidnapping Earthlings. The problem is clear. The solution is not.

—Stanton T. Friedman, retired nuclear physicist

Introduction

Serendipity brought this book's authors together several years ago, when we were living on opposite ends of the East Coast. We discovered that we had some important things in common, so when I, Kathleen, relocated to Florida, I contacted Denise, and we met in person for the first time. It wasn't long before we decided to bring our efforts together by sharing information on the alien abduction phenomenon, working jointly on several investigations, and collaborating on a new research project. Each of us had more than 18 years of experience in the field and were committed to solving the conundrum of alien abduction. Soon a seed was planted for this book, and after lengthy discussions and evidence-sharing, the seeds began to sprout and grow roots.

Denise knew me as the niece of Betty and Barney Hill, whose 1961 UFO abduction received worldwide media attention. In 1965, a violation of confidentiality brought their case to the public through a series of unauthorized newspaper articles. It was upsetting at the time, because my aunt and uncle were prominent New Hampshire residents, known as Civil Rights advocates, who didn't want their UFO experience made public. They had served on a committee, through the U.S. Office of Economic Opportunity, to establish the Rockingham County Community Action Program. My uncle was the Chairman of the Board of Directors. His outstanding involvement in Civil Rights had earned him a seat on the State of New Hampshire's State Advisory Committee for the U.S. Commission on Civil Rights.[1] In other words, they were credible individuals who did not wish to relinquish their positive public image. Later, they collaborated with John G. Fuller to tell their already known story in the 1966 best-seller, *The Interrupted Journey*. The 1975 primetime movie, *The UFO Incident*, starring James Earl Jones and Estelle Parsons, presented a partially fictionalized version of the story.

My educational background at the University of New Hampshire in social science, social research, and psychology provided excellent preparation for my current avocation. During my undergraduate years, I spent time volunteering as an intern at New Hampshire's state psychiatric hospital as part of my training in abnormal psychology. I had hoped to earn a graduate degree in psychology or clinical social work, but after graduation was faced with the responsibility of supporting myself and my first husband, while he attended graduate school full-time at the University of Cincinnati. He majored in the philosophy of psychiatry, a subject that I found fascinating and absorbed like a sponge. Pressed for money, I took the first job that I could find teaching in the Over the Rhine section. It served me well because I had the opportunity to use my skills as a social worker and to learn teaching methods through graduate work in the Education Department at the University of Cincinnati.

As my first husband neared the completion of his Master's thesis, I applied to the graduate program in school psychology, determined to eventually earn a doctorate. I was elated when the university awarded me a full scholarship and an assistantship, but there were funding cuts and the assistantship fell through. Although I had a full scholarship, I couldn't manage the financial burden of supporting myself. It was one of the major disappointments in my early life, one that propelled me into becoming a lifelong learner through independent study.

After leaving Cincinnati, I spent many years working as an educator and education services coordinator, and continued my graduate studies on a part-time basis. My research on the subject of hypnosis propelled me to make the decision to earn a certified hypnotherapist credential from the National Guild of Hypnotists. My proclivity toward scientific thought and strong background in the social sciences has served me well.

I retired from my professional career to devote full time to a topic that I consider seminal. If there was conclusive evidence that my aunt and uncle had been abducted and returned to their natural environment by extraterrestrial beings, it would be the biggest story in modern history. I had to examine every piece of evidence: the original investigation reports, the scientific analysis of the evidence, hours of hypnosis sessions with one of America's most prominent psychiatrists, Fuller's archival collection, the debunker's reports, the psychological test results, and so on. Then I conducted extensive interviews with my aunt, along the close encounter route and in her home. I became aware of information that had not previously been published and gained new, compelling insight into the case.

After my aunt's death in 2005, I invited the well-known and highly respected ufologist and retired nuclear physicist, Stanton T. Friedman, to collaborate on the book that I had been researching and writing for many years. He acted as a consultant, insuring that my statements were accurate and unbiased, and contributed additional scientific content on the investigation of a star map my aunt observed aboard the craft. After 15 years of research and investigation, my book with Stanton T. Friedman, *Captured! The Betty and Barney Hill UFO Experience* (New Page Books, 2007), was published. In 2010, our second book, *Science Was Wrong* was published. Each of us contributed seven chapters on a variety of scientific subjects that were originally declared impossible by some well-educated, powerful scientists who were wrong

Denise and I have forged the same type of relationship as UFO abduction researchers. Denise is an intelligent and highly knowledgeable abduction investigator—one of the best, in my opinion. (You will learn more about her education and professional experiences in this book.) I had marveled at the fact that she possesses information that only a few prominent abduction researchers are aware of. It is information that we hold in confidence and use to assess the probability that abduction experiencer's memories are consistent with a real event. I would later discover that Denise acquired some of these professional secrets in an unusual manner—aboard an alien spacecraft.

She confided the details of her experiences to me near the beginning of our relationship and asked me to quietly investigate her case. I spent nearly three years interviewing Denise and her family members, examining her memoirs, facilitating her memory process, perusing her medical records and evaluating her case in an unbiased manner. Due to my family's negative experiences with individuals who have a propensity to falsify the facts about any UFO or abduction case in order to promote their own negative agenda, I had cautioned Denise to retain anonymity. If I were an abduction experiencer and made the decision to go public with my information, I know that the "sharks" would have a feeding frenzy. My aunt and uncle were victims of *ad hominem* attacks and false and misleading information throughout their lifetimes. I didn't want Denise or her family members to be subjected to the worst side of some human beings.

Denise and her family had kept their alien abduction story under wraps for 30 years and now had to make the difficult decision to step forward with the truth or retreat into the safety of perpetual anonymity. There was a huge chance that Denise's exposure to the public would affect her sense of well-being. We spent the major part of a month in negotiations through e-mail and over the telephone before we made a final decision, although it was not without some trepidation. One of the witnesses had to bravely step out of the "abduction experiencer"[2] closet for the sake of many others who are now standing on the precipice, wanting so desperately to speak up, to release what is inside them, to share what they know is the truth beyond a doubt. But following considerable deliberation about the possible consequences, and with her husband's approval, Denise decided to reveal her true identity to the public.

After many years of silence, Denise's husband was willing to attempt to unlock his memories of their "missing time" experiences, first by talking about them and then through hypnosis. A few blanks were still there like black holes waiting to be filled in, if possible. Denise wanted to test her conscious recall against what her husband could remember. She had already undergone several hypnosis sessions when she resided in Colorado, but her memories were hazy and the records of her statements under hypnosis had been irretrievably lost. I agreed to facilitate Denise in her effort to unlock her memories through hypnosis, giving us a fuller understanding of her experience.

I had promised "Jennie," the second experiencer in this book, and her family an assurance of anonymity. If her identity was revealed to the public, it would all but guarantee their financial ruin and the loss of her family's status in their community. Disclosure was not an option. Yet her richly detailed memories of abduction by non-humans were too compelling not to be shared. We had to proceed by fictionalizing her story just enough to preserve her anonymity, but at the same time to share the details of her story as accurately and honestly as possible.

In addition to this, a third section had to be added to this book on the personal stories of several abduction experiencers who, like Denise and Jennie, have endured astonishing contact experiences with what, by all accounts, are extraterrestrial beings. Most have conscious memories of a close encounter with unconventional craft and observing non-human entities prior to an abduction. Their neighbors had witnessed strange lights near some of their homes. When they realized the magnitude of what was occurring in their lives, many became fearful, and certain places, objects, sounds, and lights brought on sharp recall of unearthly environments. Some have a strong desire to "tell all" about this nagging reality that has disturbed so much of their lives, but the fear of public embarrassment waits in the wings, exerting a strong hold on a person's decision to step forward with the truth. An avenue to bring these people together on common ground, without fear of ridicule or persecution by non-believers, is long overdue.

Of extreme importance to us is our yearlong research project designed to conduct a quantitative analysis on certain concurring commonalities shared by the majority of abduction experiencers. The results of the "Marden-Stoner Commonalities Among UFO Abduction Experiencers Study" are startling. Our research has led us to discover abduction experiencers who are strangers to one another, but have remarkable and highly unusual characteristics in common. Their correlating data is startling, perplexing, and begs further investigation by the scientific community. (To read the report in its entirety visit *www.kathleen-marden.com* and click on "Commonalities Study Final Report.")

The information we've collected has caused us to ask these questions: Does contact with entities from other worlds or exposure to an alien environment cause human beings to develop common illnesses? How can theoretical physics explain human procurement processes that seem scientifically impossible? How can ETs travel millions of miles across the vast expanse of space and arrive on Earth unharmed? Why do the majority of abduction experiencers develop uncommon abilities that are not found in a control group?

Our readers must be wondering why we decided to write this book and do this research now. People are asking for disclosure of the facts and the truth behind the UFO mystery. We are sitting on the very edge of discovering another piece of this puzzle. There will never be a perfect time for people to come out with their stories, yet more and more credible information is being revealed by intelligent, well-spoken, educated, down-to-earth people. The reason more people don't tell their stories is that they are pilots, firefighters, military personnel, doctors, celebrities, political figures, or other individuals who would risk having their lives and careers ruined if their identities were disclosed. It is imperative that they maintain an honorable place in our society.

The episodes in this book are real and factual, and have been well documented over an extended period of time. Some took place during daylight hours with witnesses present who were willing to swear to their written statements. We realize that some readers will look for reasons to dismantle the facts, knowing this can be done with any story presented to the public today. It was decided that no matter the reaction, these people's accounts of alien abduction are too compelling not to be told. It is our hope that this book will hold some clues people are looking for in their attempts to solve this mystery. At the very least, we look forward to receiving new information as a result of telling these people's stories.

1

Missing Time in Colorado

It was a beautiful mid-August afternoon in Arvada, Colorado, and Denise and Ed Stoner were looking forward to a weekend trip to their free-standing mobile home on the Grace Acree Ranch near Buena Vista. The Stoners, Denise's parents, and 50 other families parked their trailers year-round under the watchful eye of the ranch owner, Grace Acree. During the summer months, the Stoners routinely took weekend sojourns to their home away from home 137 miles southwest of Arvada, a suburb west of Denver.

The clear blue Arkansas River lined with smooth, gray river rocks and jagged boulders, cuts through the property. It is known worldwide for its excellent whitewater rafting. To the Stoners, it was an inviting reprieve from the hustle and bustle of the metropolitan area where they made their home. Each year, they spent approximately 20 weekends at the ranch fishing, hiking, and visiting with family and friends.

Their trailer was the last in a line of campers close to the fields and Arkansas River. They had constructed their own fireplace, table and chairs, and privy away from the ranch house that sat on the property. Though they were not far from family and friends, beyond them there was only open sky, flaxen fields, high mountain peaks, and the sound of coyotes teaching their young to howl at the moon.

Not far from their camper and next to the river were the remains of an old cabin that had been occupied nearly 100 years earlier by the first inhabitants of this tract of land, a woman named Emily and her husband. Two small graves were sheltered behind a half-fallen black iron fence, hidden among the aspens. Local legend has it that Emily's young child drowned in the river, and overcome with grief, she followed shortly thereafter, swallowed up by the roaring river's grasp.

Denise and Ed loved walking for miles in the Colorado sun, looking for arrowheads and tools the Ute people had used for a summer camp in the area before European settlers occupied the land. A railroad crossed the property not far past the gate, and once or twice a day, a train would come roaring through on its way cross-country. It broke the silence in the serene setting steeped in Native American tradition and cowboy culture. It was to be a delightful weekend getaway.

Denise's parents, accompanied by a close family friend, had gone on ahead of their children to prepare the camp for a weekend of merriment, relaxation, and fishing at the headwaters of the Arkansas River. The Stoners were expected to arrive no later than 8:30 p.m. for a dinner that was being prepared by Denise's mother. Denise had loaded the car with food, clothing, and gear with assistance from her 14-year-old disabled daughter Dienna, while Ed tended to details of his job as operations manager at a Boulder flooring business before leaving for the weekend.

The trip to their camp had become part of their weekend routine. It was 5 p.m. on Friday afternoon, August 13, 1982, when the three family members and their 6-year-old dog, Ginseng, a pure bred Shih-Tzu, piled into their blue and white Ford Granada for the drive to their campsite. Ed gassed up the car and checked the odometer near his home in Arvada. The sky was clear and traffic was light on the backroads. His eyes met a huge sign stretching across the highway that announced "Howdy Folks! Welcome to Golden—Where the West Lives." Traffic was heavier now, but he would soon pick up U.S. Highway 285, the route that led to Buena Vista. Finally, traffic thinned somewhat as they and others made their way to Conifer, Bailey, and Grant along winding mountain roads to Kenosha Pass, a 10,000-foot high cut that leads toward Jefferson and the South Park Valley on the eastern side of the Front Range. Beyond Jefferson, U.S. Highway 285 straightens, offering a more comfortable and relaxed journey across the broad basin.

View of South Park, Colorado. Licensed under Wikimedia Commons GNU Free Documentation, Public Domain, Credit: Matthew Trump

Ed always stopped on Kenosha Pass for a breather and to take in the view of the South Park Valley and the town of Jefferson at the base of the pass. The scenic overlook is about 60 miles from their Arvada home. Considering the city traffic and mountain roads, it took almost 90 minutes driving time. They arrived at approximately 6:30 p.m. and stayed at the scenic vista for not more than 10 minutes. Denise decided to stay in the car while Ed and Dienna took in the beauty of the valley below. They returned to the car, Ed taking the wheel again. The sun was still strong in the western sky, as he made a right turn and a gentle, curving arch downward and to the left toward the valley floor below. Their drive across South Park Valley to Trout Creek Pass and their encampment 7 miles north of the town of Buena Vista would take an additional 90 minutes.

While Ed wheeled the car down Kenosha Pass toward Jefferson, Denise was busy watching the mountains and the vast expanse of the valley below, while Dienna was getting sleepy in the back seat. Ed and Denise were relaxed and talking, switching topics every few minutes. Visibility was crystal clear for miles. Denise was taking in the ranchlands to her left, barren except for one new home being built not far off the road. There were never many cars on this stretch of highway in the early evening, none on this particular night.

As the Stoners began to descend from Kenosha Pass to Jefferson in the South Park Valley, Denise heard Dienna's soft, evenly spaced breathing as she slept soundly in the backseat. Ginseng was pressed up against Ed's leg, his head nestled near his knee, sound asleep. Finally, they passed through Jefferson.

Glancing into the sky, Denise's eyes were drawn to two yellow-white lights that were increasing in size and seemed to be rapidly approaching. They were 4 miles south of Jefferson when the lights were over the car. Without warning, the Stoner's vehicle began to move sideways off the highway toward the desert floor, under someone else's control. They felt momentum, but nothing more.

As if only a moment had passed, the Stoners found themselves beyond the southern end of the Mosquito Range driving up Trout Creek Pass beyond South Park Valley. They had no memory of driving through the valley or the town of Fairplay, south of Jefferson, on the stretch of US 285 that led to Buena Vista. A moment before it was broad daylight, but now the blackness of night had blanketed the valley and a penetrating chill had fallen upon the interior of their car. Somehow 40 miles of their journey had simply vanished.

Ed was mystified. Why was it dark? Who had turned on his headlights? It wasn't him. The sun had been shining only a moment earlier! The hair on the back of his neck was standing on end. Denise spoke first: "What the hell just happened?" Immediately Ed pulled the car to the side of the road and checked his watch. Although moments before it was 6:55, it was now nearly 11. He was hyperventilating, disoriented, and perplexed. His fear increased exponentially when he checked his trip odometer. It read 74 miles: the exact reading that he had taken 4 miles south of Jefferson, hours earlier. There was a major discrepancy not only in time, but in travel miles. Somehow the stretch of highway that they always traveled from Jefferson to Trout Creek Pass had not registered on the odometer or in their minds. They had lost 40 miles on the trip odometer and more than three hours had passed. Ed and Denise sat on the side of the road in silence attempting to rationalize the discrepancy. They were stunned, shaken beyond words. There was no prosaic explanation for their lost time and the missing miles. Shaking his head in disbelief, Ed proceeded up Trout Creek Pass, taking in the starry night sky to Johnson Village and Buena Vista. Seven miles beyond that was their destination, the Grace Acree Ranch.

When Ed wheeled into the ranch, he and Denise were met by a surprising site. Their family and friends were standing in the road in front of their trailer, watching to see if the headlights coming down the driveway were theirs. The anxious expressions on their faces added an additional layer of mystery to the night. What had happened? Where had they been? It was going on 11:45 p.m., more than six hours from their 5 p.m. departure time.

Ed's father-in-law and his friend had become so concerned that they were entertaining the idea of using the phone at the ranch house to call the Colorado Highway Patrol. Ed checked his trip odometer again. This time it registered 97 miles from his house in Arvada to his destination seven miles north of Buena Vista. On every preceding trip they had taken that summer, the odometer registered 137 total miles. There was a 40-mile discrepancy and no simple explanation for what had occurred. How could they explain this without sounding irrational? They offered the best explanation they could come up with: the truth.

Denise's folks initially thought that their daughter and son-in-law were kidding when they explained that they didn't know where they had been and why they were late. They razzed and teased them in a joking manner, not believing a word they said, even though they could see they were still stunned. Denise's mother, especially, insisted upon a rational explanation. It took some time for the reality that they were telling the truth to set in. She was persistent, but after a while, she realized that Denise and Ed weren't lying. They really didn't know what had happened and they were a bit shaken by it, but not so upset that they pursued an answer at that time.

The Stoners returned home after their weekend sojourn, perplexed but none the worse for wear. Denise might have considered filing a formal UFO sighting and "missing time" report, if she had known of an investigating agency, but she didn't. The U.S. Air Force had shut down Project Blue Book, its UFO investigation branch, in December

1969. Without it, the Stoners knew of nowhere to report their sighting and missing time event. Denise's full-time job with the National Park Service and the care of her daughter did not allow free time to search for answers. Ed also worked long hours at his job. Computers weren't household items in 1982, the way that they are today, so a quick Internet search for help was impossible. Still, the perplexing event weighed on Denise's mind. She was determined to eventually find an answer, but it would be nearly 30 years before she asked me to assist her in solving her mystery.

2

Anything but Extraterrestrial

Had it not closed more than a decade before her missing time incident, Denise might have filed an official sighting report with Project Blue Book, the U.S. Air Force's (USAF) official UFO investigative arm, which operated at Wright-Patterson Air Force Base from 1952 until its closure in 1969. Its first predecessor, Project Sign, was placed under the jurisdiction of the Intelligence Division of the Air Force's Air Materiel Command at Wright Field, and was given the responsibility to collect UFO reports that might be a threat to national security and distribute them to concerned agencies. In 1948, it issued an assessment of the situation, which concluded that the flying saucers are structured craft under intelligent control that could out-fly and out-maneuver U.S. and Russian aircraft, and which were probably extraterrestrial in origin. The estimate of the situation was forwarded to the Pentagon, but was subsequently ordered destroyed by the USAF's Chief of Staff Gen. Hoyt Vandenberg, after he cited his opinion that the investigators had failed to produce physical proof of extraterrestrial visitation. Subsequently, Vandenberg closed Project Sign.

In early 1949, the Air Force announced that the name "Sign" had been compromised, so a new name, Project Grudge, was given to Project Sign's successor. Grudge's mission was to devote minimal time to recording, summarizing, and evaluating. When it obtained enough data to conclude that UFOs were not a threat to national security, the project would be closed. Future reports were to be handled on a routine basis and not given a lot of attention. Grudge achieved its goal six months later when 77 percent of its 244 UFO cases were explained away as being attributable to natural phenomena, misinterpretation, or psychologically motivated. It continued to function covertly for another two years with the goal of debunking UFO sighting reports due to national security concerns. It was feared that the American public might enter into mass hysteria if an enemy planted false rumors of alien craft in U.S. airspace.

Captain Edward Ruppelt took charge of Project Grudge in 1951 and breathed new life into the program by expanding and standardizing it. UFO reports were once again taken seriously, and a directive was issued to every USAF facility in the world to immediately send information on any UFO sightings to the Air Technical Intelligence Center. In 1952, the now well-organized group was renamed Project Blue Book.

Upon Ruppelt's retirement from the Air Force in 1954, Project Blue Book downsized and came under the direction of four additional project heads before it closed in 1969. It never again enjoyed the large staff and support that it had under Ruppelt's direction. Its focus changed from the systematic documentation and investigation of UFO reports, to explaining away as many reports as possible, by any means and without serious investigation.

In 1955, the Battelle Memorial Institute in Columbus, Ohio, evaluated 3,201 UFO reports to determine whether or not they represented technological developments not known to this country and to construct a model of a UFO based upon the data. Their study, the largest one ever done for the United States Air Force, under contract to the Foreign Technology Division of the USAF in Dayton, Ohio, was titled "Project Blue Book Special Report No. 14." Each case was evaluated on several criteria and categories, including Balloon, Astronomical, Aircraft, Miscellaneous, Psychological, Insufficient Information, and Unknown. "Unknown" meant that it defied explanation as anything originating from planet Earth. In the end, 79.5 percent of the sightings were assigned to the first six categories, indicating that they had a mundane explanation, and a significant 21.5 percent fell into the "unknown" category, meaning that despite every effort to identify the UFO, it defied prosaic explanation. The cases were evaluated for quality, witness reliability, witness observational experience, sighting duration, and the distance from the witness. No report could be listed as "Unknown" unless all four final report evaluators agreed that it was a true unknown. All other categories required the agreement of only two of the evaluators.[1]

An evaluation of the data yielded the result that 31.1 percent of the "excellent" cases were assigned to the Unknown category, whereas only 3.9 percent of the Insufficient Information cases were "excellent." A full 62.5 percent of the best cases were classified as Unknown, whereas only 33.9 percent of the "doubtful" and "poor" cases were Unknowns. Clearly, the evaluators presented significant information that structured crafts for which there was no prosaic explanation were entering U.S. air space.

Despite this very significant conclusion, on October 25, 1955, the USAF issued a widely publicized official press release that contradicted the Battelle Institute's official report. Donald Quarles, the Secretary of the Air Force, stated, "On the basis of this study, we believe that no objects such as those popularly described as flying saucers have over flown the United States. I feel certain that even the unknown three percent could have been explained as conventional phenomena or illusions if more complete observational data had been available."[2] This claim was a direct contradiction of the study's findings and patently false. The evidence clearly indicates that 21.5 percent, not 3 percent, of the cases studied fell into the Unknown category, meaning that they could not be explained as conventional phenomena or psychologically generated illusions. The probability that the Unknowns were just missed knowns was less than 1 percent. Again, political expediency had overshadowed the truth. The Air Force had an "anything but extraterrestrial" agenda.

The controversy began once again in 1966, when 1,112 UFO reports were registered, and the Air Force was accused of incompetence or a cover-up. That same year, the Air Force awarded a contract to the University of Colorado for a 15-month study of the UFO problem under the Direction of Edward U. Condon, PhD, a physicist and theoretician at the University of Colorado. Condon was member of the National Academy of Sciences and had served as the Director of the National

Bureau of Standards for the federal government. He named Robert Low, the Assistant Dean at the Graduate School, as his assistant and project coordinator.

Nearly from its inception, the project was plagued with charges of misconduct. Although Condon was ostensibly chosen for his eminence and his lack of any stated position on UFOs, it soon became apparent to overseers that he held a negative position on UFO reality. Critics alleged that Edward Condon avoided cases that warranted serious attention and clearly presented a negative tone in his statements to the media. His negative bias became clear as a bell when he presented the biggest crackpot cases of alien-human contact he could find, drawing uproarious laughter from his audiences.

Partway through the project, a scandal threatened to blow the Condon Study wide open, when a staff investigator working for the project discovered the infamous "Trick Memo," written by Robert Low, Project Coordinator, on August 9, 1966, and handed it to David Saunders, the Co-Principal Investigator for the Condon Committee. It read, in part:

> In order to undertake such a project, one would have to approach it objectively. That is, one has to admit the possibility that such things as UFOs exist. It is not respectable to give serious consideration to such a possibility.... The very act of admitting these possibilities just as possibilities puts us beyond the pale.... The trick would be, I think to describe the project so that, to the public, it would appear a totally objective study but, to the scientific community, would present the image of a group of nonbelievers trying their best to be objective but having an almost zero expectation of finding a saucer.[3]

He went on to suggest that social scientists could attract funding for the academic study of UFO witnesses.

David Saunders was terminated because of statements he made about Robert Low's "Trick Memo." Somehow the memo made its way to John G. Fuller, a journalist who published information about the scandal in an article titled " Flying Saucer Fiasco: The Extraordinary Story of the Half-Million Dollar 'Trick' to Make Americans Believe the Condon Committee Was Conducting an Objective Investigation" in the

May 14, 1966, issue of *Look* magazine. Saunders and R. Roger Harkin's book *UFOs? Yes!: Where the Condon Committee Went Wrong*, was published the same year. In the book, Saunders and Harkin stated that it had become apparent that Robert Low was primarily concerned with "building the record"[4] following his successful negotiation for the project, and in March 1967, made the decision to announce to the team on a confidential basis that it would fail in its effort to support the extraterrestrial hypothesis even after it had searched diligently for confirmatory information.

At the project's conclusion, Edward Condon ignored the scientific evidence for UFO reality and issued the statement, "Our general conclusion is that nothing has come from the study of UFOs in the past 21 years that has added to scientific knowledge.... We consider that it is safe to assume that no ILE [intelligent life elsewhere] outside of our solar system has any possibility of visiting earth in the next 10,000 years."[5] This statement was issued despite the fact that a significant number of compelling best-evidence cases examined by the Condon Committee defied prosaic explanation.

The Condon Committee's findings were quickly reviewed and approved by the National Academy of Sciences, which issued the announcement that "The least likely explanation for UFOs is the hypotheses of extraterrestrial visitations by intelligent beings."[6] The evidence indicates that there was never a concerted effort to conduct an unbiased investigation of the UFO problem. This finding eventually led to the Air Force's decision to close Project Blue Book in 1969. Observers protested Condon's statements, claiming that the number of Unknowns should have been higher. They argued that some of the unexplained cases were so puzzling to the reviewers, they had difficulty denying the reality of unconventional flying objects.

Despite the official statement made by Edward Condon that the committee found no evidence of extraterrestrial visitation by intelligent beings, a follow-up study of the evidence by the special UFO subcommittee of the American Institute of Aeronautics and Astronautics found that 30 percent of the 117 cases studied in detail could not be identified after all possible explanations had been exhausted.

Today, more than 43 years after Project Blue Book closed its doors, the official veil of secrecy continues to shroud UFO reality. The mainstream media avoids it all together, or writes it off as a product of the popular imagination, misinterpretations of various conventional objects, or hoaxes. News anchors donning aluminum foil hats chuckle nervously when events like the Phoenix lights or the Chicago O'Hare Airport multiple witness sightings of UFOs occur. Abduction experiencers are assailed with *ad hominem* attacks or dismissed as being fantasy-prone or too scientifically naive to realize they are experiencing sleep anomalies. When highly credible government officials and retired military officers gather to present their personal experiences with extraterrestrial craft and to debate the issue of a government cover-up, the story is usually avoided by mainstream newspapers. For example, on September 22, 2012, the National Atomic Testing Museum in Las Vegas hosted a panel discussion on UFOs. The panel of distinguished experts included Col. John Alexander, a former military insider who created Advanced Theoretical Physics, a group of government officials and scientists brought together to study UFOs; Col. Bill Coleman, former Chief Public Affairs Officer for the USAF; Col. Robert Friend, USAF Project Blue Book Director (1958–1963); Col. Charles Halt, Deputy Base Commander at RAF Bentwaters AFB in England who witnessed UFOs close-up in December 1980; and Nick Pope of the U.K. Ministry of Defense. All participants had retired from their positions in the government and felt that they could speak freely on the topic. The group was brought together because each member is thought of as highly credible. Each formerly held a high position in the military or government.

With regard to the UFO cover-up, Col. Charles Halt stated:

I'm firmly convinced there's an agency, and there is an effort to suppress.... I've heard many people say that it's time for the government to appoint an agency to investigate.... Folks, there *is* an agency, a very close-held, compartmentalized agency that's been investigating this for years, and there's a very active role played by many of our intelligence agencies that probably don't even know the details of what happens once they collect the data and forward it. In the last couple of years, the British have released a ton of information, but has anybody ever seen what their conclusions were or heard anything about Bentwaters officially? When the documents were released, the timeframe when I was involved in the incident is missing—it's gone missing. Nothing else is missing.[7]

Colonel Alexander disagreed with Col. Halt, stating that although he believes that UFOs are real and constitute a global phenomenon, his extensive search has produced no evidence of a government cover-up. Nick Pope seemed circumspect in his assessment of the situation, when he explained that though the UFO field has its "fair share of crackpots, charlatans and cultists,"[8] the panelists were employed by the government and military, and therefore are considered credible. He stated that, in 1951, the British were faced with a wave of sightings that were witnessed by RAF pilots and tracked on radar after it had declared that UFOs are only misidentifications, hoaxes, and delusions unworthy of investigation. But despite the official denial, the MOD continued to investigate UFOs and covertly kept a close watch on reports from the "UFO community."

Pope's statement about crackpots, charlatans, and cultists came after September 19, 2012, when Lord Martin Rees, the U.K. Astronomer Royal, proclaimed, "If aliens had made the great effort to traverse interstellar distances to come here, they wouldn't just meet a few well-known cranks, make a few circles in corn fields and go away again."[9] His authoritative claim was made in complete ignorance of the evidence. To the contrary, his compatriot, Nick Pope, argued that the UFO subject is worthy of proper scientific research, especially when one has photos, videos, and radar. "It's unscientific to ignore data simply because it doesn't fit your worldview," he said.[10]

Colonel Bill Coleman presented a firsthand account of his close encounter with a circular object that he termed a flying saucer. He and Colonel Robert Friend, who was Project Blue Book's last director, stated that they were both aware of UFO reality. Friend declared that he was opposed to Project Blue Book's closure in 1969, adding, "My primary explanation for these things is that, yes, they're real, and I think it would be much better if the government or some other agency was to take on these things and to pursue the scientific aspects of it.... UFO sightings are real, and you will not be ridiculed by any honest organization that investigates it. Just come forward, quote your case and allow people to investigate what they can to make some determination about what it is that you've seen. In the future, just remember that we're on your side."[11]

The distinguished panel's revelations deserved attention by mainstream media outlets, but it was largely ignored. The Huffington Post covered the story, but it was relegated to the paper's "Weird News" section. With our propensity to ignore credible experts and relegate them to the category of kooks and cranks, is it any wonder that most witnesses fail to come forward with their sighting reports? When UFO reality is flatly denied by government officials and the conservative scientific community, is it any wonder that UFO abduction experiencers hesitate in coming forward? Some social scientists claim that alien abduction can be easily explained as sleep paralysis, sleep hallucinations, fantasy, misinterpretation, and hoaxes by attention seekers. American society tolerates adult bullies who launch *ad hominem* attacks upon UFO witnesses and abduction experiencers. For these reasons, it's not surprising that Denise Stoner remained quiet about her missing-time experience for nearly 30 years.

●　●　●　●　●　●　●　●　●　●　●　●　●　●

3

Meet the Stoners

I met Denise Stoner not long after my husband and I relocated from New Hampshire to Central Florida in 2009. I knew of her outstanding reputation as Florida MUFON's State Section Director and Chief Investigator, and we had corresponded from time to time via e-mail, although I had never met her in person. She was a very active UFO and abduction investigator who hosted regularly scheduled meetings for the interested public and for abduction experiencers. I informed Denise of my interest in her work and this initiated an enduring professional relationship. She is currently Florida MUFON's Assistant Director of Abduction Studies under my supervision, having retired from her former MUFON positions, and hosts the UFORCOP Florida Research Group.

Denise and Ed have enjoyed a stable, harmonious marriage for nearly 50 years and are the parents of an adult disabled daughter, who resides with them. They are family oriented and enjoy spending time with their large, nearby extended family. They also have long term, enduring friendships with a variety of people.

Ed strikes me as a quiet, pleasant, industrious fellow of above average intelligence. He was born in the Bronx and lived there until age two, when his parents divorced. His mother later remarried, and he was raised by his mother and stepfather, who worked in the aerospace industry. Due to his stepfather's job transfers, he grew up in central

Ed, Dienna, and Denise Stoner in the late 1970s.
Credit: Olan Mills Portrait Studios.

Florida, Pennsylvania, and California. Ed met Denise in California while home on leave from the Army.

His father was a medical doctor with a practice in Oviedo, Florida, and later had a large part in starting the medical athletic department at the University of Central Florida. He was a member of "The Flying Doctors," and was president of the Florida Academy of Family Physicians. During his career he had many other titles.

Ed's mother attended an art school early on, and later went to a modeling school, as well as a beauty college in Las Vegas. He describes her as, "an extremely beautiful woman with a bubbly personality who loved her family." Ed spent a great deal of time with his grandparents in Pennsylvania (his grandfather was an optometrist), and later on with his father, stepmother, and grandparents in Florida.

After his service to his country, he took advantage of the G.I. Bill and began his college studies at Western State College in Gunnison, Colorado. He had intended to complete his studies, but his daughter had been born with cerebral palsy, and her medical care placed additional financial demands upon him to become a full-time breadwinner. Throughout his career, he has worked as the general manager and operations manager for retail flooring companies. Eventually, he opened his own business which he ran successfully for a few years, until he decided to slow down and assist a former coworker in establishing his own business. He was then employed at the business until his retirement in 2012.

Denise also hails from an educated family. While still in her early thirties, her grandmother had immigrated to the United States from Scotland, along with her husband, a man who was 10 years her senior. Both were college-educated and had worked as schoolteachers before coming to the United States. Neither held the credentials necessary to teach in the United States, so Denise's grandmother found employment at a well-known retail chain in Hartford, Connecticut. She quickly moved up to a management position. Denise's grandfather managed a huge estate whose grounds had been designed by someone who worked for the National Park Service.

Denise wrote of her grandparents:

My years growing up were so very special. The town in New England would remind anyone of a Norman Rockwell painting. Neighbors were friendly. The first home my parents owned was on Fenwick Street in Hartford, Connecticut, where I lived until I was ready for first grade. When my grandfather was not working, he was my constant companion. I miss him as much today as I did the day he was gone from this earth at age 88. He was a proud Scottish gentleman who read to me, taught me to tie my shoes, took me on my bicycle to a bus stop with a bench I called the 'Yellow Seat' where I insisted he tell me the story of 'Jack and the Beanstalk' over and over. It was my favorite story and he never tired of telling it to me or at least let on that he was. We had a permanent close bond long after I married and left home. The same feelings existed with my grandmother but she worked long hours and was not at home as much. I live today by the many quotes she whispered to me or wrote in my diary to help me get along with people I would encounter in my life. I considered her beautiful inside and out and never wanted to disappoint either of my grandparents by being anything other than what they had shown me by example people should be.

Denise also had a close bond with her parents, as is evidenced by the following passage:

My Dad was a hard worker who was working six days a week in an auto repair shop, coming home to take courses toward his dream job working in the aerospace industry. My Mom stayed at home during our early years and saw to it that we had time with family, friends, singing lessons, piano lessons, dance lessons although she had gone to college.

My sister and I modeled clothes on TV for the department store my grandmother worked for and did some early commercials that were shown live. We had closets full of the newest dresses but never felt spoiled. We knew that hard work went in to obtaining those items for us. My parents purchased a beautiful new Cape Cod style home when I was in first grade where we could ice skate on a pond together in the winter and swim in the summer with all the other children in the town. My science teacher was actually a lifeguard there during the summer months. I also was the oldest of 13 cousins, and they were all in nearby towns. My uncle was a baseball coach for a very well known team and had played himself years before.

My sister was a talented pianist, and our teachers recognized that early. I struggled with it so I enjoyed playing mostly for myself. My dad's mother was a very talented pianist also and played for groups of people in restaurants, veteran's homes, etc. and was always the one who played for hours at our holiday parties. Neighbors gathered around the piano singing all the songs of the era. She and my grandfather ran a large dairy farm in Colchester, Connecticut.

When I began high school, our home in this quiet New England town sold, and we moved to Florida so my dad could interview for jobs in the aerospace field. After several weeks, my cousin in Sacramento contacted him and said we should come out west, as my dad would be able to obtain a job at Aero Jet where my cousin worked. We did that, and I was soon ensconced in this new state to begin a whole different type of life. I had to make different friends and was very shy.

It helped a great deal when my parents purchased a beautiful home near my second cousin, and I knew I would be attending school at a brand new high school just being finished. I would be in the first graduating class. This excited me as all the students would be new and starting fresh together. It turned out I had many friends, many dates, and close girlfriends I am still in touch with today. My family unit has always been strong and that has never changed. I consider that I had a perfect childhood.

Denise and Ed married young, the summer after Denise's junior year in high school, nearly a year after Ed entered into military service. She became a war bride and completed high school while Ed fought in Vietnam. He returned home safely the September after her high school graduation and they began their life together on a military base in the southeastern United States. After Ed's honorable discharge, the couple set their sights on Colorado, where Ed would go to college first while Denise worked. Then it would be her turn. By chance, Denise's parents were planning to sell their home in California and move to Colorado Springs, so they would be nearby. Denise and her parents had a close, supportive relationship, and she had missed them during her time as a military wife.

The couple made up their minds that Denver, being a large city, would give Denise the best opportunity to find a job. Additionally, there were many good colleges to choose from and Ed could make use of the G.I. Bill. But Denver presented many challenges that they hadn't anticipated. The city was expensive and Denise's job opportunities were not lucrative enough to support herself and Ed. He too had to find employment, at least temporarily, until he was able to attend college. Soon Denise discovered she was pregnant and could no longer work. After a long and difficult labor, her first and only child was born, with cerebral palsy. The challenge of raising a disabled newborn coupled with Denise's inability to work outside the home brought on a financial crisis. Living in the city became more and more difficult. They had a child to raise now, and they had to balance their financial obligations with the cost of living and Ed's desire to complete his college education.

They made the decision to leave Denver, but remain in Colorado. Ed found Western State College, a small state school high in the mountains in a town that had only two main crossroads. The cost of living was within their budget, and Ed was accepted as a matriculating student. So, off they went. They were still young, healthy, and excited about their new adventure, and luck was with them. Not long after they drove into town, they met a man who suggested they take a look at a building that used to be an old ski lodge. He had moved it away from its original location near the river and converted it into affordable apartments for students. Denise and Ed loved the location away from town, on a piece of property by itself, and took advantage of the offer.

Soon settled in, Ed began his classes, while Denise offered her services as a babysitter for the students who had babies and attended classes during the day. Although she was happy in her marriage and her life with Ed and their young daughter, there was something in her new environment that gave her an uncomfortable feeling. It was difficult to make the adjustment to the limitations of living in Gunnison, a tiny village in the mountains, after residing in an urban environment for most of her adult life. Services were limited, making it difficult for a young couple with a disabled child who needed extensive medical services.

The feeling grew until once and for all they made the decision that they should leave; they would be better off in a large city with all of its services and conveniences. Despite their financial concerns, they returned to the big city of Denver. There was a sense of urgency now, because they had wasted another few years. It was already the 1970s, and life had to move on proactively.

So, this young couple left town once again. This time they would remain in the big city for many years. Ed made several attempts to re-enter school and complete his college education, but the challenges of supporting a wife and disabled daughter, plus staggering medical expenses, made it impossible. Cerebral palsy and the complications that came with it required physical therapy, occupational therapy, and speech therapy at least once a week for years. At the time, they did not have medical insurance, so they put every extra penny toward Dienna's care, plus what they could get in assistance from private charities.

Ed's college courses in economics and business landed him a job with a floor covering store as the youngest man they had ever hired. They personally trained him in business and sales, giving him the skills he needed to move up in the company, and paid for his training courses. Then they groomed him to be a general manager for several of their stores. According to Ed, it was "the school of hard knocks...until I opened my own store...in Florida."

Despite her many challenges, Denise graduated from Barnes Business College in Denver. Later on, her professional growth classes, in topics such as dealing with difficult people, recognizing personality types, dealing with stress, and relaxation techniques, prepared her to teach stress reduction for more than 12 years to professionals in such fields as medicine and law. She is also a certified hypnotist specializing in regressive hypnosis and is a certified scuba diving instructor.

For 12 years, Denise did background investigations for the military on recruits seeking highly classified clearances for work on nuclear submarines. Prior to retirement, Denise moved to a military research facility where she was the training coordinator for several hundred military and civilian employees. Before this, Denise spent eight years with the National Park Service in Denver, where she worked on a team who did the planning, design, and construction for the first national park in Saudi Arabia. As part of her job responsibilities, she responded to Congressional inquiries and wrote from draft to final form for engineers, scientists, and historians on historic studies, proposals for historic monuments, and trail brochures. She won several monetary awards for her outstanding work. Her retirement from the Federal Government allowed her to expand her work on UFO research and investigation.

She began her hypnosis research in Denver, during the 1980s, under the direction of Dr. Bob Romack, by volunteering to participate in one of his experimental studies. They worked together for five years on pain control, smoking cessation, and past-life regression research. Denise also worked as a paranormal investigator with abduction experiencers that reported the presence of spirits in their homes following what was believed to be alien visitation. As part of her investigation, she documented evidence of new psychic abilities in abduction experiencers that had not been present previously. She also volunteered on a research team with Dr. Romack, studying abductees' abilities to locate missing people and predict future events.

• • • • • • • • • • • • • •

4

Research Begins and Memories Emerge

In my role as an abduction researcher, I had to make an unbiased assessment of Denise's claim. To do so, I had to collect all the evidence and obtain statements from all of the surviving witnesses, in addition to speaking directly to Denise about her experience.

Denise appeared to be genuinely perplexed by her memory of unconventional lights traveling rapidly toward the vehicle that she and her family were riding in on the night of August 13, 1982. She consciously recalled that the puzzling lights rapidly descended in their direction. Almost immediately, the car seemed to slide sideways off the highway. There was no accident and there were no injuries. Ed had not lost control of the vehicle. In the blink of an eye, the Stoners discovered that they had traveled 40 miles that didn't register on the odometer that Ed had been checking. They had no memory of passing through Jefferson or Fairplay, on the stretch of US 285 that led to Buena Vista. They arrived at their destination hours later than anticipated.

Having completed my preliminary interview with Denise, my next step was to speak to her mother, a petite, pleasant 80-year-old woman who resides near Denise. I had the opportunity to question her at one of Denise's private meetings for abduction experiencers. She reassured me that she clearly remembered the concern that she felt when her daughter, son-in-law, and granddaughter failed to arrive at their family's weekend enclave on a ranch near Buena Vista. She also mentioned a perplexing childhood experience that might have been UFO related.

45

Later, she presented me with a signed statement attesting to her memories of the event on August 13, 1982. She wrote as follows:

9/14/2012

I am Denise's Mom and Ed's Mother-in-Law. During the late summer of 1982 I was waiting at our family weekend and vacation camp area on a ranch just outside Buena Vista, Colorado for Ed and Denise to arrive with their daughter. They always arrived on time so we never had to worry unnecessarily. We drove in earlier from Colorado Springs on another route while they came from Denver.

They were supposed to arrive at approximately 8:15 to 8:20 and when that time had passed along with 3 more hours, Denise's Dad and our longtime family friend became very worried. We all discussed going up to the ranch house to use the only phone to call the police to see if there had been an accident. The guys actually wanted to get in the car to start driving the route back to Denver to look for Ed's car.

We were at a loss and began to walk down the dirt road from camp towards the ranch house knowing we were going to awaken the elderly woman who was the long time care taker of the ranch. Too much time had passed and Ed knew the phone number so would have stopped somewhere to call unless they were stuck in the middle of nowhere but even then at some point a highway patrol or cross country trucker would pass an automobile in trouble. Everyone was willing to help back then especially a stranded driver in the dark.

Just as we reached the turn in the road, the three of us spotted headlights in the distance turning on to the ranch road. It was only minutes before we knew it was Ed's car. They pulled up and rolled down the window. We walked back to their trailer and asked them what happened. Denise and Ed were confused because they realized it was so late, they had no explanation for their lateness. Denise's Dad teased, our friend did the same. I always had to have an answer when it came to this type of thing and needed to know what was going on. They insisted they had no idea why they were so late and were searching for an answer themselves. I am not good with secrets and thought if they were keeping one; this was not a good time to do so.

This is what I recall about that night.

Una Kent

Given her mother's confirmation of the late arrival, I interviewed Denise's husband and took a statement from their daughter, and requested signed statements from family members outlining their memories of the night in question. All agreed that a perplexing missing time event had taken place for which they could not offer a prosaic explanation.

Next, I studied a map of Colorado and determined the travel time for each section of their route. I had resided on Colorado's Western Slope for several years and traveled through the Trout Creek Pass to the South Park Valley and up Kenosha Pass on my way to Denver. Only three years ago, I drove along Route 285 from Denver to Buena Vista and beyond, to visit an old friend on the Western Slope, so I was familiar with the terrain in this sparsely populated area of Colorado.

Descending south from Kenosha Pass to the South Park Valley floor treats drivers to a breathtaking view of a sprawling expanse of valley abundant in natural resources. Snow-capped peaks and mountain chains line the valley in every direction. The valley is relatively flat from the base of Kenosha Pass and the town of Jefferson south to Fairplay and Hartsel, an incorporated town founded in 1880, along the banks of the South Platte River and near the geographical center of Colorado. From Hartsel, it is approximately a 13-mile drive to the base of Trout Creek Pass (9,487 feet). Mapquest lists the driving distance from Jefferson to Trout Creek Pass at 38.09 miles, approximately a 37 minute drive. The 53.26 mile drive from Jefferson to Buena Vista takes about 55 minutes.

August 13, 1982, was a clear night in the South Park Valley with a temperature of approximately 64 degrees Fahrenheit. There was no measurable wind. The official temperature readings registered a high of 72 degrees and a low of 43. Twilight began at 7:44 and the sun set at 8:03. The moon that night was 36 percent illuminated, and its last quarter had been the day before. It rose at 2:23 a.m. and set at 2:41 p.m.[1] When we take into account the Stoner's departure time, distance, and route, along with the favorable weather conditions, I could find no prosaic explanations for their mysterious "lost" period of time. It was also clear to me that the Stoners were attempting to present an honest account of their experience as possible, even when there were minor discrepancies in their individual statements. This is normal and indicates that they had not conspired to develop a totally consistent story.

My next step was to assess the Stoner's biographical and emotional history. Had they lived a relatively stable life? Did they have a long-standing history of emotional stability? Had they reached the anticipated level of achievement considering their educational levels and background? Were they attention-seekers? Were they fantasy prone? There was much to be evaluated.

As I got to know Denise, I was impressed by her serious involvement in UFO studies. Her volunteer work for the Mutual UFO Network was thorough, efficient, and highly professional. She took her position as Florida's Chief UFO Investigator, State Section Director, and Field Investigator seriously. It became clear to me that she possessed none of the negative personality characteristics that would cause me to suspect that she had a personality disorder or was merely seeking 15 minutes of fame. She and her husband had met with success in their lives, and enjoyed emotional and financial stability. She maintained a neat, well-kept home; her life was well ordered and meaningful; she was cool, calm and serious, but also had a good sense of humor. Additionally, Ed Stoner had written and signed an affidavit outlining his memories of the night of August 13, 1982. His account matched Denise's in correlating detail.

As we discussed her case in further detail, Denise mentioned to me that she had undergone regressive hypnosis with Dr. Romack, the doctor that she had assisted in Denver. He had been the first hypnotherapist to assist her in recovering memories of her missing time experience in the South Park Valley on the night of August 13, 1982. When I inquired about her memory of the missing time event, Denise wrote:

> I only recalled being taken off the road into the desert, the light following above us, and a figure of some kind standing in the shadows near the car. That is all we ever accomplished although, I rattled off some information about a "Black Hole Theory" that made not an ounce of sense to either of us when I awoke. Dr. Romack was writing that down as fast as he could, when he realized what I was saying. He was going to put it in a book and passed away before he ever began writing. He told

me some of what I said, as I did not recall any of it when I woke up. We were both amazed and surprised at the information gleaned from some entity in a ship who stated their mode of travel had something to do with a Black Hole.

It is interesting to me as an investigator and researcher that Denise had forgotten most of what she remembered in Dr. Romack's office. Additionally, she did not have copies of the recordings of the statements she made under hypnosis and there was no existing written record of the memories that emerged through hypnosis. When she asked me to facilitate her memory recovery, I agreed to assist her, with the reservation that her preexisting knowledge of alien abduction might color some of her memories. I would use my advanced training in hypnosis to reduce this possibility.

Hypnotic regression is an important tool for memory retrieval, but the hypnotist must safeguard against the possibility that the hypnotized person might construct false memories where no real memories exist. It is extremely important not to ask leading questions, as while under hypnosis, a subject is prone to fill in the blanks with false information. Patience is required. I prefer a forensic hypnosis technique—used widely by police departments—which requires the use of carefully worded questions that discourage the construction of false information. One must supply a minimal amount of information to the witness. For example, you might consider asking "Was anyone else with you?" instead of "Was your daughter in the car with you?" It is also common practice to ask a leading question as a "verifier" to test whether or not you can lead the witness, such as "Can you describe the light fixtures that you saw on the craft?" It is also important to instruct the witness that he or she should recall only the events that *really* happened.[2]

Forensic hypnosis gained notoriety in 1976 when a California bus driver and 27 students on the bus were kidnapped and buried alive. The driver escaped and led the police to the children, who were released to their parents. The bus driver underwent forensic hypnosis and remembered the license plate number of the kidnappers' van. This led to the arrest and successful prosecution of the criminals.[3]

After we discussed my views on hypnosis, I inquired as to Denise's reason for requesting that I assist her in facilitating her memory. She told me that this was her longest period of missing time and the only one for which she had family members and additional witnesses who could verify that she and her family were hours late in arriving at their destination on August 13, 1982. She wrote:

> I always remembered it and replayed it in my mind many times. Although this is not the only episode when I was wide awake, it was important to me as an adult, as it appears to cancel out all the standard myths such as sleep paralysis, lack of witnesses, no UFO sighting, bedroom occurrence, etc. I thought that we could uncover the full story from A to Z with no missing entries giving us the complete picture of an abduction experience. I did not want to begin with a partial picture that could possibly be explained away.

On July 7, 2011, Denise and I met for her first hypnosis session. Prior to the hypnotic induction, we reviewed Denise's medical and hypnosis history, and her reason for wanting to revisit the 1982 event with hypnosis for memory enhancement. She stated that she had observed, in the distance, three yellow-white lights in the sky as the family was beginning to descend down from Kenosha Pass to Jefferson in the South Park Valley. She recalled that beyond Jefferson, the car seemed to slide sideways although her husband seemed unaware that anything was wrong. Her daughter was sleeping soundly in the backseat. Her next memory was of suddenly finding herself on Trout Creek Pass with no memory of the interim 40 mile stretch of road.

Denise stated that when they arrived at the campground, her family members, who had been expecting her arrival, had grown concerned and were discussing driving north along their route to search for them. Although they were 3 hours late, their odometer didn't indicate the anticipated driving distance.

Denise was very attentive at listening to and following my suggestions. She had very good concentration skills and responded very easily. I offered her suggestions to return to August 13, 1982, and provided a safety zone that she could retreat to if she became uncomfortable with her memories.

Kathleen: Can you remember your trip to your camper on the river near Buena Vista?

Denise: Yes. It was Friday evening during the second week in August. Ed was driving our Ford Grenada. It was blue with a white roof.

K: Was anyone else with you, or were you and Ed alone?

D: Dee Dee was in the back seat, and our dog was with us, too.

K: How old was Dee Dee?

D: She was a teenager.

[Denise's memory was not as sharp as I desired, so I offered suggestions for additional clarity and focus.]

D: Dee Dee was getting sleepy in the backseat. Ed and I were relaxed and talking about a variety of subjects...just talking on and on and switching topics every few minutes.

K: Go on...you can remember everything. Tell me what you see.

D: We're on the other side of the pass [Kenosha], driving down to the valley. There are three big lights off in the valley. They are coming down to the valley floor. They don't look right... there are no roads out there.

K: Can you describe them?

D: The lights are huge...bright white. They appear to be rotating slowly. They are attached to another object. It looks like two convex mirrors. They are rounded and the ends are touching...like two round plates with their rims touching. It has tiny specks or bumps all over it.

K: How can you see it so clearly?

D: It is right above my head. It is below the mountains. The car starts to move sideways. I look to see if it is waking Dee Dee up. It's not.

K: Where are you in relation to the lights?

D: I am in the valley under the plates. It's funny...the three lights can separate from the plates and they can stay in the sky. The lights come down to the ground. I'm supposed to go into the center of the lights.

K: Are you alone?

D: I feel like there is someone else there but I can't see them.

K: Do you see anything?

D: I see like a glob of clear, lighted, jelly-like substance...like the size of two of my heads maybe, floating to me. And I looked up and I saw a black obsidian-colored opening that was shaped like an hour glass. And the craft was now really low to the ground, but I couldn't have just stepped into it. There was no opening other than this hour glass...I could see the hour glass. I knew I had to step into this gel and I was afraid to, but I knew that I was going to have to do that. And I did. I stepped into it and as I started to step in, and as soon as I got an arm and a leg in, cause I reached out to touch, I was sucked into it. You didn't go partway in. You did all or nothing. So I was sucked in, and when I did, I felt like I was breaking up—like I was shattering is the only way to describe it. And then a voice said, "You'll be alright. We're going in now."

[I detect tension in Denise's voice, so I offer calming suggestions.]

D: And the opening was too small to fit a human body through it and it didn't matter if you weighed 90 pounds or 500 pounds, you would not fit in the opening. And so we went through, and I remember, because I had all of my thought processes, this is a little painful. And so it kind of went shooo [makes sound] up in through and the very minute that I got inside this craft, I was me again, and I don't remember the process or the change...and the gel was gone. It was gone...not a trace of it. And it [craft's interior] was not shiny silver. It was a brushed...maybe the lightest silvery titanium color...maybe. Not much lighter than this opening, and it closed over or I couldn't see where it was anymore—that opening. And I looked up and started to look around and the lighting was real dim. I couldn't see where it was coming from. And it didn't seem...well the floor to ceiling was taller than me, but not a lot I don't think.

K: How bright was the light?

D: Not very bright. It was almost like as you look up along where the wall meets the ceiling...that's where the light came from. And it was a thin line. And whatever would show from that and maybe the same in a couple of other places. And so whatever glow would emanate from that is what lit that area. Nothing from the floor...nothing from the walls...and so they were lined up here. I almost want to say there might have been something sticking out from the wall. And I don't know if it was a jut out that went all the way down or if it was a type of a railing affair, but there was something. It wasn't a smooth wall to the floor.

K: Did you see any fixtures or furniture or that type of thing? [This is a bit leading, but necessary.]

D: No, unless this thing in the wall had anything to do with some working mechanism of some sort. I don't know. I don't know what was around the corner. I don't know where the entrance was. It disappeared. And all along this hallway were Greys. And something in my head said those are soldiers. And I didn't think anything of it and they were just looking straight ahead. Not moving...not saying anything...just standing there. And then there was a door a little ways down to my right but around the corner at the curve of the hallway came this entity. He's one with eyes...the ones that blink vertically. He came to me and bent over and cocked his head sideways and put his face right in mine and said, "We have to go in."

[Denise is becoming tense, so I offer calming suggestions and question her about the entities in the hallway.]

K: The row of entities that you mentioned seeing as you entered the craft...Do you remember what they looked like and how they were dressed, if they were dressed?

D: No clothes. There was not a crease or a line or a separation between the skin. They looked like the Grey that was more blue than gray standing on the desert floor, only darker.

K: Do you have any idea how tall they were?

D: Yeah. Probably the top of their head came to my shoulder and I was 5 feet, 5 1/2 inches tall then. They were under five feet. They were well-formed, well-shaped with great big eyes.

K: What color?

D: Black, I think. Very dark. They were kind of misty. They almost blended into the titanium...silvery shade of the wall. Almost. Yet I knew they were there, but it wasn't a shadow. You know, you would say were they standing in a shadow or part of the wall? But no...they were figures standing.

K: Are you thinking anything?

D: I think, what are these? They are figures of some kind— bulbous heads, slender, no clothes. One wears a belt—almost like a military belt with maybe an insignia, but I can't remember it now.

K: That's okay. We'll go back to that later. Relax and be at ease. It will all come back to you now. You'll remember everything, and you'll be able to tell me everything.

D: One steps out, and I know I'm supposed to go into the next room. Uh, uh. No. I feel I need to go back to the car. And I'm told I will be alright. I feel anxiety and yet familiar. There is something familiar about it.

[Denise starts to breathe heavily, her voice quivers, and her body trembles. I offer calming suggestions and comfort her.]

K: It won't hurt you now. Just stay calm. Relaxed. Very relaxed and at ease.

D: There is a tall one—3 or 4 feet taller than the others.

K: Is he taller or shorter than you?

D: He's taller than I am. He doesn't look like the others. He's a little more upsetting. His head's not attached to his shoulders in the same way. His eyes go straight up and down near the sides of his face. He has no nose. He has a tiny very red mouth when he opens it. But he doesn't talk. I hear him. He's very intelligent. I tell him not to touch me. I repeat that I want to go back to the car. He's not going to take me back until he's through.

[Denise is showing signs of becoming distressed. She continues to breathe heavily and her body quivers.]

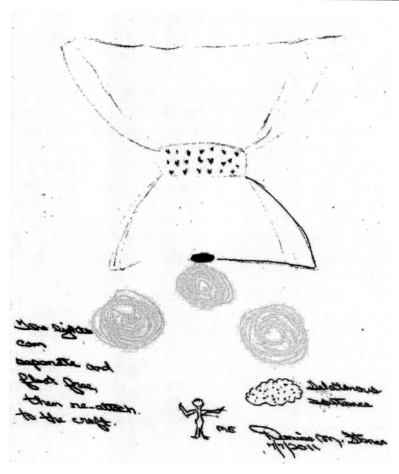

Denise's sketch of the UFO.

K: Remember Denise, if you want to go to your safety zone, you can do so at any time. It is your decision. You don't have to go on if you don't want to. You can wake up if you wish. It is entirely up to you.

D: Yes, I think I want to go back.

I then guided Denise back to the present and offered post-hypnotic suggestions to remember only what she is comfortable with, and stress that she doesn't have to remember anything that causes anxiety or fear. In addition to this, I suggested that her memory of the event, if it was a real event, would become clearer over time as long as it didn't trouble her too much. I advise her to call me immediately if she experiences discomfort. I then counted her out of hypnosis and gave suggestions that she'd feel energized and comfortable.

When she was fully awake, I asked Denise to sketch the craft that she had observed. She complied with my request and drew two tea cup–shaped handle-less objects connected in the center by a speckled ring. The bottom cup faced downward and the top cup was upright. A small black hole marked the center of the bottom cup/craft. Three large, yellow balls floated in a triangular pattern below the craft. Denise noted that they can separate and float free or attach to the craft. She placed herself on the ground under the craft. She also sketched a speckled gelatinous substance that was slightly larger than she was and was located to her left.

I was surprised by Denise's sketch. It was unlike any that I had ever received. The hourglass-shaped craft and the gelatinous substance that was used to transport her aboard the craft were not consistent with other reports of which I was aware. Several experiencers had informed me that they were placed into a vat of gelatinous substance or a viscous fluid during their experience aboard the craft, but this was unique and different. I had to consider the possibility that she might have been filling in information when a real memory couldn't be accessed. To this day it remains uncertain to me.

On July 8, Denise wrote the following message to me:

I wanted to let you know since the hypnosis, I find that I am not thinking of the taller entity on the craft as much as I am the craft as it approached over my head and that strange substance. I was not afraid of that, and since I have known about UFOs for many years and retained some memories of them, I felt my heart rate pick up but more in excitement and curiosity than anything else. It isn't until I face that odd entity that concern and an element of fear creeps in, although I have a clear memory now of being a part of that substance and floating upward. The only way to describe it remains that I felt I was a part of the substance and had separated into it somehow. I still feel he—I just know it was male—was a highly intelligent being even though the appearance was so ugly and frightening in our terms. I do want to know what was about to happen so plan to move forward as we are able. I hope much more will open up at least on this particular craft.

Denise and I met for a second hypnosis session on October 26, 2011. She informed me that, during the past three months, she had recalled more information about her missing time experience. She stated:

I clearly remember the car that we were traveling in with my husband and my daughter through the valley in Colorado, South Park...I now remember exactly where we were...part way through the park headed for Trout Creek Pass and Buena Vista where we were going to go to our camp area to meet my parents. And the car swept...I saw the lights...I still didn't know what they were at the time. But I saw the lights off to the left in the valley and pointed them out. And then the car was swept off into the desert-type land and it didn't drag. It lifted but only the tires were not in the dirt...in the sand, so I think that the car was only off the ground about 2 or 3 inches and it just moved sideways...not rapidly. Possibly, if I had to put a speed on it... about 30 miles an hour? It just went sideways, and it went up past the only ranch that was sitting not too far off the highway up towards some rolling hills...foothills. And then I remember seeing the craft that had one part of it going clockwise and one counterclockwise with the center piece being still. I don't have a memory of how I got out of the car. But I'm pretty sure now that my husband and my daughter stayed in the car. I'm not positive, but I think so. And I was standing then under the craft and there was an entity, which was a Grey, more bluish than gray colored.

Denise and I reviewed the detailed information that she provided during her first hypnosis session. She had processed and integrated the information that had come to the forefront in her first session and was beginning to remember many previously repressed memories of the missing time event. She was ready to recall the memories of the tall being that had previously been too frightening to recall comfortably. I asked Denise to proceed from where she stopped the last time.

Denise: He's [the tall figure] going to take me into the room. I heard a voice—a mechanical male voice. He's very intelligent. There are more entities in the room—five or six of them. They look like the ones in the hallway except some of them are taller. He wants me up on the table. He says it's going to be just fine. I ask him what he's going to do. He said it's a test.

Kathy: I see. What happened next?

D: I'm wearing jeans and a sweatshirt and a tee shirt underneath. He tears the cuff of my jeans by my right ankle because he's going to put a wire on the top of my foot. It's thin and it stings. [Denise winces, so I offer the suggestion that she won't feel it now.] He puts it in the vein. He says he's going to leave it there for a while. I ask him why, and he says so that the ones on Earth will be able to recognize me easily. That's all I need to know. I ask if it will always hurt, and he says no. It will stop hurting.

K: Go on.

D: He does something to my left eye. Something comes from behind me. He puts something that feels like a piece of sand into my tear duct. He says it will fall out in a few days. It was on the end of pinchers. He pushed on my abdomen with something flat. It was diamond shaped [Pink and approximately 2" × 3"]. He pushed over my ovaries, and it burned. He said, "That will be all." I ask the purpose and he says "It is not for you to know. You are a part of the whole." I felt some fear. He makes me know that he has seen me for a long time. He shows me a screen on the wall. He's tracing a thing on my mouth—so this will stay sealed until the time is right...until the others come forward.

K: Can you describe the screen on the wall?

D: It's almost like a platinum tube. It goes round and round—like he's spinning something. It came up from the floor and it's not even a screen. It's like...there was no stand or nothing solid... nothing solid. A 3-D image just rose up off the floor. There was no actual item. Just the image came up off the floor. But I had to look slightly down into it. I see earth, only there are no lights. I see only rust colored countries and deep midnight blue water.

He shows me a dark planet and we are going back to it. He just shows me a planet...far, far...it's not in our solar system.

K: How does he impart that message to you?

D: He shows me our galaxy. I can see it. He shows me our solar system and then he points. I see it in that thing...

K: What thing is that?

D: The thing that he brings up on the floor. He shows me our galaxy and our solar system, and he points out on the edge.

K: The edge of what?

D: The edge of our galaxy.

I was very cautious not to lead Denise. Therefore, I did not ask specific questions that might induce a subjective opinion or fantasized information called up to please me. When she had come to the end of her narrative, I asked her to describe the tall entity in great detail if, and only if, she could remember the descriptive details. She responded as follows:

His eyes are yellow. They have a black center and lines running through them. I can't see his mouth. He has 3 long fingers and a thumb. One didn't work well. He used it as pinchers a lot. His fingers were very long and his palm was small. He had an oddly jointed body. He appeared to be skin and bones and his joints looked arthritic. They were bulbous. I didn't see his knee caps. His head swiveled. He was wearing a dark jacket that extended to his legs. It had a stand-up collar like a priest wears with piping.

Her description of the entity sounds very much like what is commonly known as a praying mantis or insectoid being.

I brought the hypnosis session to a conclusion and engaged Denise in a conscious interview. Knowing that the details brought out through hypnosis have an increased probability of being fantasy-based, I felt more comfortable speaking to Denise in a full waking state. I hoped that she would be able to rely upon her memories of the event and that this would reduce her chance of confabulating.

Denise: I saw a lot more this time. The room was very oddly shaped...like an old-fashioned camper that used to be very narrow on the back side and come up like this...straight down. The floor was odd and I wish I knew what was odd about it. I couldn't get it that clearly.

Kathleen: You said that the examiner was so tall that he had to bend over. How tall do you think he was?

D: I think 7 or 8 feet. And he always was hunched over. It reminded me of the MRI machine. And I now know that he put a wire in this [left] foot and right up this [left] side.

K: You told me about something that was done to your eye?

D: Yes, my left eye...the tear duct.

K: What do you remember about that?

D: I remember a tiny little white bead and something coming over the top, and they put it inside...way in there. [Denise described what might have been the insertion of an ocular implant.]

K: Can you describe that equipment to me?

D: I remember what it looked like. It looked like metal or stainless steel pinchers with a point at the end, and they had the little thing on the end. And when they pulled it out, the white thing was gone. So, I assumed it was in my tear duct or in my eye.

K: Do you remember anything else about it?

D: It had like pinchers or pliers, but very, very high-tech looking. They were very small...very, very fine and small. You wouldn't even know that there were two parts to it until it got really close to your eye. The white was whiter than a pearl and perfectly round. White, white, white, white.

K: How large was it? Can you compare it to something that you can think of?

D: It was a little larger than the tip of a pencil, about the size of one of the stones in my ring.

K: So, a little larger than a poppy seed?

D: Yes, a little bit larger than a poppy seed...because it hurt going in. It was just real quick. It kind of popped into the tear duct. And I didn't know what that was for at that time.

Denise's sketch of the insectoid entity she observed (left) and artist Stephan Smith's rendition of the entity Denise described (right).

K: You were talking about the examiner's skin. It was what color?

D: It was bumpy, and it was a greenish. It had a green tint to it... tan. And in between all of the bumps it was darker.

K: It was just bumpy?

D: That's the only way I could describe it. I wanted it not to be bumpy, because the times I felt it, it didn't feel bumpy.

K: Was there a pattern to those bumps?

D: Yes, they were all the same all over with the darker in between and then kind of a little bit of dark...mottled. That was it. They didn't look bumpy, but had a mottled look, because it is wasn't veins or the funny appearance of the iris where you can see different colors...

K: When he touched you, how did it feel?

D: Slightly rough.

K: Was there any temperature difference that you noticed?

D: Yes, but not much...slightly cool.

K: Soft? Hard?

D: It was firm. That is the word I would use. It was firm. I had a feeling or an instant where I sensed that this person could be very controlling, and could be mean...could be cruel...without any feelings or emotions about it. He was doing kind of what he had to do. If I stepped out of bounds, I really wouldn't matter to him. So, the idea of being taken...that's where the fear came in. Like just do what he says, and it's going to happen anyway, so it was kind of like a business relationship. Almost...?

K: You said that you didn't notice any facial expression. Did he express any emotion?

D: No. I got the feeling once or twice...the way he would cock his head was like...what? I'm curious about that. If you want to call that emotion, that's how he was.

K: Maybe as you remember more and more, you'll gain enough information to know more about what's going on.

Denise and I met again on November 4, 2011. She wanted to explore her medical examination in greater detail. I wanted to compare her memories during this session with what she had stated previously, to look for signs of fantasy material or confabulation. The following is a transcript of her statements.

Kathleen: You can go back to the craft now, Denise. Find yourself back on the craft. And I'd like you to tell me everything you can remember. Recall everything that you observed; everything that you did; everything that anyone else did. You can begin.

Denise: The doctor—the insect- or lizard-type—has completed the tests. [Denise was still uncertain about the ET type that she had interacted with.]

K: Can you tell me about those tests?

D: He put a small object in my eye. It's going to be there for a while. He did something to my ovaries.

K: What did he do?

D: That was painful. He put something into my abdomen and said that...It's almost like I was impregnated, but I wouldn't be the incubator.

K: Do you see what it looks like?

D: I've seen a needle that is used for amniocentesis. It is very similar to that.

K: Where exactly did he put it?

D: Very close to the center of my navel...into my navel. [I've heard this many times. It dates back as far as my aunt, Betty Hill's testimony.]

K: Did he tell you what he was doing that for?

D: He just said that this is for you to carry but not to incubate for long...and that's all.

K: To carry but not to incubate?

D: Not for long.

K: Not for long. How did he get to your navel? [Denise had told me the last time that she was fully dressed, so I wanted to ascertain whether or not her memory remained consistent.]

D: Yes. I was wearing jeans, and he unbuttoned and unzipped the jeans. The jeans were opened, and they were pulled back to expose my navel. My shirt was up.

K: Did you feel any sensation when he did this?

D: Pain. It really hurt.

K: It won't hurt now. Okay, you can forget about that.

D: It hurt more than the wire in my foot. And it burned. It spread underneath and it burned.

K: Did you tell him that he was hurting you?

D: Yes. I just asked him to stop. I said stop, because it burns, and the taller of the Greys came over and touched the side of my temples and said, "It will be all right now." And it stopped hurting. Or I thought that.

K: You thought it?

D: Yes, I think so.

K: Did he communicate with you in any way aside from touching your temples?

D: I can't tell where that information came from. It was.... It won't hurt anymore. It's all right now. It won't hurt anymore. I don't know if the doctor is saying that or who is.

K: Did the voice have a sound?

D: Very odd. I couldn't tell if it was male or female.

K: Did it sound like a human voice? Did you see any humans in the room? [I offer these suggestions to see if I can lead Denise to confabulate false information, or if she will stick to her story.]

D: No. The Grey had fingers on my temples and something went through my temples on both sides, and it stopped the pain.

K: What did it feel like? How did you know that something went through your temples?

D: It was like a current of some kind. There was no pain. It was a very peaceful sensation. It's almost like it interfered with the pain.

K: Were there any other tests?

D: No. I, um, felt like this was directly into my uterus or close. And I said, "I'm carrying something? What am I carrying?" He didn't answer. He just responded, "There are others that stay. Look for the little larger, round eyes...larger than yours...a little larger...larger shaped eyes and they're kinder than us. But you get to keep them."

K: Did he tell you anything else about this?

D: We try to breed more loving...he didn't say loving but that's what he meant...more loving than us and we need that.

K: Go on, you can tell me what you remember.

D: I ask him...I'm not sure...I asked him if we're moving. He said no, because I would get sick...because I wouldn't tolerate the feeling...that this craft is operated mainly biologically. Biologically...that's what he said. It's how it's powered, and I feel a fear because now it's slightly strange.

K: How do you know this?

D: He takes me into a room. It's connected to the center of the craft and the outer rim. It has its own atmosphere.

K: The room has its own atmosphere?

D: Yes.

K: What does it feel like?

D: I stepped into this room and there was a total change in the atmosphere. And it's slightly...It feels like it wants to spin but it's not.

K: What do you see in the room?

D: It's blackness, and it's cold. But I don't believe that it's solid. It's so black. There's a pole and in the center of the pole there's a device...mechanical and there is something wrapped around it. Then there are two arms that come out, and they vaguely resemble the accordion tubing from a dryer...maybe. And they come out from that and then go down to a flat plate. But then it's the interior that's alive. You just know that it's alive and the whole thing inside that center block is in motion. It can think. It operates the craft. It runs the craft.

K: Where did you see this? Was that in the examining room that you were in? [Again I attempt to lead Denise to tell me it was in the examining room in order to test her.]

D: No. He took me out further down the hall and he said, "I'm going to show you the center of the craft. It's capable of shielding itself...of protecting itself...of passing through anything that flying through space can toss at it. It can pass through time... time. It could not do this until a few years ago." This is something they just, in their time, recently developed. It's not...I'm not feeling the fear, but at the time it was very frightening.

K: Did you express fear at that time?

D: Yes.

K: Did he respond to that?

D: He said I would never be able to understand the enormity of what he was showing me. This entity brought them here in it. This biological machine brought them here in it. I asked if there was a console and a point of operation. Did he have to operate this from any point in this thing? I didn't have a word for it. I felt disoriented. The room makes you feel disoriented.

And he said, "Not any longer. It is a thought process. And that is new also. And now we must take you back. Oh, it's affecting your muscles." He said I must leave. [Denise's body starts to jump around and her limbs thrash about as if she is being hit by pulse waves.]

K: You can relax now. Your muscles won't jump anymore. You can leave. You're getting out of there...getting out of there. You're calming down. You're calming down. You're calming down. You're very relaxed now...very, very relaxed. Your muscles will no longer jump. Take a deep breath in and release it. You're very calm...very calm and collected. Your muscles won't jump anymore. [Denise calms down.] Now think about the time that your muscles jumped. Did you feel any physical sensation when that was occurring?

D: Yes.

K: What was it?

D: Like I was being hit with something I couldn't see.

K: Go on with your story.

D: It's time to prepare for the exit. So, I'm glad to leave that room, and I feel I came out of something that was pressurized. Like I was in something that was bouncing me back and forth... externally.

K: What happens now that the pressure is gone?

D: We walk down the hall, and I don't see anyone. No one...none of the other entities.

K: Which entity are you with at this point?

D: The doctor. He said I didn't have much time left after being in that room that operates the craft. He said since I was exposed to that atmosphere I could fit through the opening to exit the craft if I'd give him that opportunity. Now the taller of the Greys has come. I'm told if I'm willing that I can get through the opening, because it will work without the substance. He stands behind me...puts his hands on my shoulders...and I touch the desert floor.

K: Your body jumped a little bit. What were you experiencing as you were moving to the desert floor?

D: I couldn't breathe and that's all I remember. It was like the wind had been knocked out of me. I could have been under water holding my breath. And I don't see the entity or the craft. [Denise pauses.] It's moved away. I see the craft.

K: Can you describe the craft? What did the craft look like?

D: I see the bottom and the middle rim holds it together. There are two parts and one rotates clockwise and the other rotates counterclockwise. The whole center section is the entity that operates the craft. It is the center disk. There are lots of lights. They are white, and there are some around the edges and on the bottom. They are yellow and there is some red and they actually rotate and rotate until they blend together until you can't tell the colors. It confuses people on the ground as to whether or not it is an aircraft. There is some green. I see the green but it's mostly white...yellowish white. It kind of looks like stained glass up front when you are up close.

K: Do you remember how you got back to your car?

D: There's a part missing, because I just find myself sitting in the seat with my feet on the ground and the door open. And then I put my feet in and the door closes. And I cannot find how we are suddenly at the top of the pass. But we are. And I turn to look at Ed, and we begin to know that something is not right, and we don't know how we got there. We start to look at the odometer that he had set. And we look at our watches. And it should be just twilight. But it's pitch black outside. And we start to figure out that something is really wrong...knowing that my parents would be looking for us. We start to talk and ask each other what just happened. We remembered coming down into the little town of Jefferson at the foot of the hill. And we came through Jefferson, and we were talking about everyday things, and then I said, what are those lights?...He looked. He remembered looking. And then we have no other memory. And we are wondering why not? And we are discussing that my parents must be worried. And my daughter is still sleeping in the back seat, and our little dog is between us up front, sound asleep. It is so dark. He checks the odometer again and kind of bangs on the glass. He wonders if it is working or if it's broken. I knew that he set it. We had a purpose for setting it that night.

This ended Denise's hypnosis session. As I began to reflect upon her startling memories of being in an alien environment and the detailed information that she recovered, I wondered if this was in fact an "artifactual" memory of information that had come her way as an abduction researcher. She reassured me that she had never read or heard this information. Still I felt compelled to speculate whether or not it was a product of her imagination. However, I had used all of my skills as a hypnotist to reduce the possibility that she might manufacture false information. Many of her descriptive details were consistent with my knowledge of the interior of a spacecraft. Her description of the ETs fit the mold. Although I was aware of information pertaining to the biological nature of the craft's central core, I remained skeptical. I was impressed by Denise's descriptive details and the fact that her body had responded to their room's environment. I had to consider the possibility that this might be real. But if it is real, many more issues are raised. What are the ethical values of beings that would produce a biological entity encased in the central core of a craft? Does it have a soul? Is it bio-mechanical, a living computer?

I had spoken with several experiencers that have memories of the craft as a living entity. One experiencer stated, "Biological material is used deep within the energy system of the craft." Another wrote to me in a private communication, "These craft are living entities, much like a bacteria. They live, breathe, function, and create. They are grown from what was initially a hybrid framework. The craft are generic, genetically modified structures. Not all craft have individual operators, but there are certain parts of their DNA replicated." Still another wrote, "The craft seems to have its own intelligence. It can sense its surroundings." This information had not been publicized, yet Denise described little-known information that others had shared anonymously with me. Perhaps the ETs were passing information to us with regard to their advanced technology—technology that seems nearly impossible to us.

In order to clear up questions about Ed's memory of the experience, I asked him to undergo a short hypnosis session with me. He cautioned me that he has never been a receptive hypnotic subject but was willing to attempt it. I was pleased that he was able to relax and easily accept my suggestions. His memory of the drive from Arvada to Kenosha Pass was crystal clear and wonderfully detailed. Everything was proceeding as normal when he drove through Jefferson. As Ed is "driving and driving," he thinks that Denise is drawing his attention to a house under construction on the left side of the road. This is the instant when Denise states that she was actually pointing out lights rapidly approaching their car. Suddenly, he becomes disoriented and senses that his car has stopped, but he feels momentum and sees swirling dust-like particles surrounding his car, as if he is in a vortex. He hears a high-pitched, pulsing whine and feels weightless, as if he is detached from his body. He is paralyzed, and his head is full of "random, spinning, analyzing" thoughts. He finds himself in a new environment and sees a smooth, "dull, reflective" domed ceiling overhead. This description is similar to Denise's description of the examining room on the craft. He is now only sensing a feeling of detachment and waiting for an extended period of time. He doesn't know where Denise and Dienna are. Finally, he hears a frequency in the tenor range that reminds him of loud tinnitus. There is a heavy pulsation, and he feels frightened and cold. His weight returns, and he finds himself clinging to his steering wheel. It is suddenly dark outside, and he is freezing. His headlights are on, but he hadn't turned them on. He realizes that he is half way up Trout Creek Pass. It is nearly 11 p.m., and Denise is "freaking out." They stop for a few minutes to gather their thoughts and attempt to discern what had just happened to them. Neither could explain it.

I had assured Ed in advance that I wouldn't push him for additional information beyond a brief and hopefully comfortable glimpse into his experience. It would have been tempting to obtain additional information about his time aboard the craft—or wherever he was—but I complied with his wishes. His emotional well-being was first on my list of priorities.

Ed's sharp memory was essential in corroborating Denise's statements pertaining to their lost-time event and filled in missing details nicely. After 30 years, the couple was finally able to gain a better understanding of what occurred during their missing time on August 13, 1982. Their UFO encounter was the first of many that they would share. After spending many years in Colorado, the Stoners moved to Florida and, as you will see in the next chapter, their missing-time events continued.

5

Missing Time
in Florida

Not long after Denise and Ed relocated from Colorado to central Florida, Denise discovered that scuba diving was a popular sport in the Sunshine State. For her, it would be a new adventure and a challenge, one that she was looking forward to pursuing. Ed was apprehensive about this new exploit, but he knew that Denise would need a diving partner, so he joined her in registering to take a beginner level course in underwater diving. Their classes made such an impression on them, that soon they had advanced up to the instructor level and were taking students into the wonderfully mysterious underwater world in both fresh and salt water diving.

A few years later, the Stoners were ready to become even more professional in this sport, so they trained in cavern diving, then cave diving, using mixed gas. At the time, Denise was one of very few women willing to attempt this type of training. When Denise went with Ed, she was the only woman among all the men diving the caves. Women dove with her in the caverns, but would not venture into this dangerous arena of total darkness and complete silence. It required an exercise in controlled panic and the ability to self-rescue if your partner could not help you. The Stoners found that they loved the challenge and began to take weekend sojourns to Florida's deepest caves whenever they could.

The best cave diving was just outside Branford, Florida, approximately 50 miles north of Gainesville in the northwest part of the state, known as "The Spring Diving Capitol of the World." Weekend after weekend, Denise and Ed drove the three-hour trip to dive the beautiful caves. The underground aquifer was inviting, and each area was different from the next. The Stoners had made many friends that shared their passion for cave diving, so it became a social event as well.

Denise's job as a training coordinator in a military research facility that developed new weaponry was particularly demanding, so on the weekend of October 19–20, 1991, she was especially anxious to disappear beneath the earth's surface to enjoy the unusual animals that lived in this special, totally quiet environment. Above all, she enjoyed exploring the fossilized walls, millions of years old, yet never touched by human hands. Divers can catch sight of fossils in the walls and those that have washed free from the limestone. Sea biscuits (the original sand dollar), still perfect and at least 15,000 years old, protrude from the ceiling and walls. There are even rare sharks' teeth from the Megladon, the ancestor of the Great White.

This particular weekend, Denise wanted to concentrate on her favorite dive spot, one of the deepest, on Little River, just off the Suwannee River. They were on the last dive of the day and knew they would have to decompress for at least 45 minutes before exiting. Line arrows on the wall pointed the way out, and the swift flow of the water allowed them to drift effortlessly back to the entrance.

Above ground, they had parked their car behind a wood, split-rail fence in the parking lot for the divers. It was a rugged area in the wilderness, with no amenities. At the end of the dive, everyone would strip off their dive gear, wash it down in the river, then change behind large beach towels or in their trucks.

The divers always stayed at a motel in a central location, the Steamboat Dive Inn, a short drive to the pristine underwater caverns. As the Stoners pulled from the parking lot in their brown Dodge D-100 pickup truck and headed for their motel, they were reminiscing about the wonders of the two dives they had done that day. They had discovered many interesting branches in each cave that could be traversed. They were now looking forward to relaxing and chatting about their day of diving at Nell's restaurant, just north of the motel.

It would take approximately 15 minutes to reach their destination. There were no road signs to guide them to and from the dive spot, so the Stoners had learned to use landmarks, such as churches, farms, and houses, to find their way. They had done this so many times that they had become familiar with the route, knowing what landmarks they would encounter next.

It was twilight and the Stoners were in no hurry. They were simply taking in the sites and enjoying their time together away from the busy city. They hadn't encountered another vehicle along the sparsely traveled road. Diving tends to stimulate one's appetite, so they were looking forward to a nice buffet dinner after they had hung up their dive gear to dry.

After they dined on fried chicken at Nell's, they turned in for the night, anticipating their last dive of the weekend on Sunday morning. All was going according to plan until Saturday night when, in the middle of the night, Denise rose from her bed, feeling compelled to leave the motel and drive to a remote location. She was able to recall bits and pieces of information—a water tower, flashing lights, sitting in the driver's seat of Ed's truck—but the rest remained a mystery. In an attempt to clear up questions pertaining to the event, Denise underwent hypnosis to sharpen her memory of that fateful night. She is an excellent hypnotic subject and quickly returned to the night in question. First, we reviewed her memories of Saturday's events. As we moved through Saturday evening, Denise became aware of rising uncharacteristically in the middle of the night and driving to a remote location. She stated:

> I had gone out by myself from the motel in Branford and something made me just leave. I never would go out by myself. And I did. I got out of bed and I left. I got in the truck, and I backed up, and I went to the right, and I took the first right. The town was shut down. It was dark. I drove not very long until there was a little spot where I could pull over. It was a little dirt road, maybe. I pulled in between the trees. I kept telling myself I was going to think. I pulled in, and I thought I saw a small opening in the trees, and I thought I saw a semi-truck with a tandem trailer or a very odd looking water tower, because it was low to the ground. It was on like bricks or stilts, and it was wide like a tractor trailer and squat. I had the wheel of the truck and pulled myself forward and stared through the windshield. And

then the top rose up on the water tower, and I realized it wasn't a water tower.

It was all by starlight. I had turned off my headlights. There was no traffic in the town. It was the middle of the night. I was staring and wondering what was going on. I wasn't afraid. I was a little uncomfortable. And then a panel opened. I realized then that the water tower had a door and it wasn't a water tower. There was ramp to a door and a ramp...somehow. And there was an entity standing on the ramp. It was one of the strange ones with the funny legs. And it stood on the top of the ramp and sent two of the small [Grey] figures for me.

I am taken out of the car and up the ramp, and he tells me this will be brief. But he has something he has to give me. He's taking me into a little room and there is nothing in the room but an odd-looking chair. And I feel like I'm in a bit of a daze or a dreamy-type feeling, because I feel floaty. And I sit down. And he takes something that resembles a staple gun almost that's attached to the side of the chair. And I ask him what he's going to do. And he says that it will just be a second. And right here he punches it. [Denise points to the left side of the top of her head.] I said what are you trying to do to me? He said that will be all.

It felt like he stapled me or something. And they escorted me off and I got into my car... Everything's dark. It's black except for a gray diamond with no points on the ends—rounded ends and a bright red light at the left and right points. Bright, bright red points and two skinny antenna like things at the top point... And it started to spin...spinning, spinning, spinning... and it spun so fast that it looked like a multifaceted crystal. Then there was a dark black circle around the outside of it. It lifted up and took off to the left and up. I feel like it had just left me somewhere. It brought me back.

And I don't really remember driving back but I was sitting in my car for a while—maybe 15 minutes. And I got back to the motel, and I went in and got into bed. I even think I was in my pajamas. When I lay down I felt my head, and it was bleeding. It was split open. I looked in the mirror at the motel, and I had a split. I tried to figure out what they had done...why they had stamped my head like that and split it open.

I checked Denise's head and found a small scar in the exact spot that she had pointed to.

Denise and Ed rose the following morning and prepared for their final dive of the weekend. Heading north on SR 129, they were approaching a small farm on the right immediately before their left turn onto CR 248, the road that would lead them to their dive spot. But something had changed since the last time she saw it. Her eyes were drawn to a new addition at the back of the barn. Several oddly shaped objects were lined up against the wall, nearly hidden from her view. Perplexed and curious, she implored Ed to bring the car to a halt and look toward the farm. Her eyes fixated upon four triangular-shaped objects. They appeared to be covered with some sort of flimsy-looking, netlike apparatus.

Denise extended her arm, pointed and asked, "What on earth are those things?" Ed, according to Denise, quickly replied that they were chicken coops. She disagreed, stating that the structures were markedly different than chicken coops, and urged him to take a closer look.

Abruptly, all conversation ceased. Then, according to Denise's testimony, they suddenly found themselves on a new road in a different location. A moment before they were in front of a small farm traveling along a familiar route to their dive spot, but now they were approaching a city next to the interstate highway that would lead them home. Somehow, they had traveled nearly 28 miles in what seemed like an instant. Feeling strange, Denise advised Ed that they were in Lake City. Ed did not respond but looked from side to side, and then replied that he was not sure where they were, or how they got there. Totally perplexed, the couple began to search for a highway marker. Not too far up the road, they found one.

This revelation seemed impossible. They were headed in the right direction when they left the motel and had been watching all the familiar landmarks. They had done this many, many times before. What had happened this time? They were slightly disoriented, and their heads felt odd. In addition to that, their watches indicated 30 minutes had

Ed (top) and Denise's (bottom) sketches of the objects in the Branford, Florida, field.

passed. The only thing they could do was head back to Branford and to the Little River Spring, totally perplexed and shaking their heads.

Arriving back near their destination, they headed north toward the four-way stop and the farmer's barn. This time, they slowed their pick-up truck and purposely perused the back side of the barn in an effort to identify the objects in the rear. Not only were there no triangular-shaped objects covered with netting this time, there were no chicken coops. They reasoned that objects as large as the ones they saw could not be moved in the amount of time they had been gone.

Denise felt terribly uncomfortable with what happened and slightly fearful. Where were they during the time they could not account for? But again, she did not know where to report it, or if that would be a wise thing to do.

The skeptic in all of us will cause us to pause and ask who or what is doing this. Is Denise experiencing a psychological aberration? Could it somehow be related to her cave diving? Is there something weird about this part of Florida? Or did all these things happen just as she remembered them? Now that I had recorded Denise's statements about two possible UFO abduction attempts and enhanced her memory of one, it was time to question Ed.

When I received Ed's statement detailing his memories of the perplexing event, I was astonished to find that his memory of the day's events were so clear in his mind. He wrote:

My wife Denise and I were trained SCUBA instructors and cave divers with the National Speleological Society, Cave Diving Section. As cave divers with hundreds of cave dives logged in Florida and in other countries, we have special comprehensive training and experience. Beyond the golden rules of cave diving is mental conditioning far beyond what an average person experiences in life. Time management, distance management, gas management, to name just a few. Every moment we are in the cave system our lives depend on this critical awareness of who we are, where we are, where we have been, where we are going. This is a mental drill like you experience nowhere on earth until you find yourself one thousand or more feet from the closest exit and one source of life, air.

We had just spent the night in Branford, Florida, all our cave gear packed and inventoried for the dive in Little River Spring just outside of Branford. We started out of town on SR 129 toward our turnoff onto CR 248 that takes us to the spring. The trip wasn't our first—according to my log book it was our 23rd dive at this spring.

It wasn't long before I spotted my turnoff ahead, when Denise said, "Look at those strange things in the field," pointing to our right. I looked to where she was pointing and saw strange shiny metal objects that came to a point; this memory lasted about one second.

I looked ahead and saw a sign I-75; you could see it coming up in the distance. I was just this side of Lake City driving on SR 247, a total of about 28 miles in the wrong direction and on a different road than where I was a second before. Approximately 30 minutes had passed since spotting the objects in the field off of SR 129. I pulled over to the side of the road with that same feeling going through me as I felt that night years ago driving to camp from my home in Arvada, Colorado. This time my wife said "It just happened to us again" both of us were scared and sat in silence. No we are not cave diving but driving a car. My time distance kicks in—wrong road, wrong place, and wrong time. If we had been underwater and these same factors were present the answer would be death, by losing one's route in the labyrinth below.

We drove all the way back to Branford on SR 247 and in Branford took a right onto SR 129 retracing our trip to that field with the strange objects. They were gone.

Our dive went well and was uneventful.

The skeptic in me must question whether or not there is prosaic explanation for the time lapse. Hypothetically, if Ed and Denise had left the Steamboat Dive Inn early in the morning, in their sleepy state, fatigue could have altered their perception. Is it possible that Ed simply made the wrong turn and drove 30 minutes in the wrong direction? But he and Denise had spent the night at the motel numerous times before and were well aware of the route that led to their dive spot. Ed

Ed's sketch of his route in Branford, Florida, to the
Little River Spring dive site.

had already driven the same route 23 times.[1] I wondered if Ed could have accidently turned onto SR 147, until I learned that he and Denise always had breakfast at Nell's and then returned to the motel for their gear. With a hearty breakfast and a few cups of coffee under their belts, it is unlikely that they would have accidently turned right onto SR 147, without noticing their error.

Ed's sketch of his route to Little River Spring indicates that he was heading north on SR 129 from the Steamboat Dive Inn, where he and Denise had spent the night. It is located at the corners of Highway 20/27 and 129. Earlier that day, they stopped for breakfast at Nell's Restaurant approximately .46 miles north of the motel on SR 129 and .19 miles north State Road 247, the route to Lake City.[2] Ed stated that he drove north only minutes before he passed the farm and the perplexing objects in the field on his right. He had intended to turn left (west) onto County Road 248 to Little River Spring a few hundred feet north of the small farm. The question that begs an answer is how Ed could have observed the objects in the field nearly 3 miles north of the turnoff to Lake City, but immediately find himself approaching I-75 near Lake City? He is certain that he didn't turn his car around. He is certain that he didn't head south on State Road 129 and take a left turn onto State Road 247. Denise is also certain of this.

Their sketches of the objects in the field in front of the farm match in detail, although they drew the objects in separate rooms. Their individual descriptions of the objects match in detail, although they had not discussed the specific features they observed.

I had to consider all of the possibilities and either accept the Stoners' story or reject it. More investigation was required. I took I-75 to Lake City and headed southwest on SR 147 toward Branford. The stretch along SR 247 is largely unpopulated forest and agricultural land, dotted sporadically with small concrete block or brick structures, and mobile homes. When I reached the intersection of SR 129 in Branford, I headed south to the Steamboat Dive Inn, a small motel located at the intersection of SRs 129 and 27. Turning around, I passed SR 247 (to Lake City), four blocks north of the motel. I was more convinced than ever that Ed couldn't have accidently made this turn. Nell's restaurant is no longer in business, but was on the right side of SR 129 not far from the turnoff to Lake City. Proceeding north on SR 129, I soon left Branford's small downtown area and traveled toward the city's outskirts. Once again, I found myself in a sparsely populated agricultural area. It is less than 3 miles from Nell's to the farm and turnoff to Little River Springs. I turned left onto CR 248 and drove a few hundred yards before I made the decision to turn around. Heading east on CR 248, I stopped at the same stop sign that Denise and Ed had stopped at numerous times that year (1991) and looked toward the small farm on the opposite side of the street just south of my location. An electrical transmission substation was highly visible. Beyond it, I caught a glimpse of the farmhouse and field. I had to turn right and head south for a better view of the small, one-story farmhouse near the road, the barn, and a constellation of small outbuildings to the left and behind it. The vacant field where the Stoners observed the strange triangular objects is to the left of the barn.

I requested additional information from Ed and Denise that might assist me in piecing together any clues that might lead to the answer to this ballooning mystery. Ed located his dive log book and sent me the following entry: "Every dive was logged and I have it in my cave diving log book as Cave #103, #23 Little River, Sunday October 20th 1991, start 11am, gas 2900 lbs, exit gas 650 lbs Exploration 600' into the Florida room via mud tunnel. Return Serpentine passage. Total decompression 25 minutes. NOTES: Lost Time (Nothing else just a reminder in my log)"

Ed's note indicating lost time is a significant clue. We now know that a missing-time event occurred on Sunday, October 20. Ed and Denise always drove from Branford to their home, near Orlando, on Sunday afternoon, as they had to work the following day. This information confirms that the missing time event took place on Sunday morning.

I hoped that a hypnosis session with Ed would fill in any missing details about the missing-time event. He was able to reach a deep level of hypnosis and seemed to be reliving the day's events. We reviewed his day diving at the Little River Spring on Saturday, October 19 and his drive back to the motel. It was uneventful. We then moved to his early morning activities at the Steamboat Dive Inn. He and Denise had an early breakfast at Nell's. Upon returning to the motel, they packed their gear into the bed of their 4-year-old Dodge D-100 brown pickup truck and closed the lid. He recalled the order in which he loaded the equipment into the truck and the struggle he had with a carpet that was bunching up. They inventoried their gear before leaving. Finally in the cab and ready to go, he headed north on his familiar route to Little River Spring, passing by SR 247 to Lake City and passing through downtown Branford. But something mystifying occured along the way. Denise drew his attention to some unusual pointed, silver-topped objects in the field that hadn't been there the previous day. He easily recalled seeing the six or seven objects in the field and automatically turned his head in their direction.

Suddenly, everything became dark, and he sensed that he was in a vacuum. It was completely quiet. He found himself in an unfamiliar location, still in his truck, and Denise was no longer in the passenger's seat. He shook his head and seemed bewildered stating, "Something's not right. It's dark." He began to hyperventilate and asked, "How'd we get here? This isn't right."

Moving ahead in time, Ed uttered an ooooh sound, indicating wonderment and surprise. He said he saw the passenger door open and a tall thin figure, approximately 6 feet tall, with Denise in its "long skinny arms." It leaned down and literally dropped Denise onto the seat. The greenish-gray non-human entity looked up at Ed. The eyes, he said, are actually paler than the skin, and the entire being had an opaque appearance, as if it was clothed in a full body suit. There was no mouth to speak of and no nose. The head was not large or bulbous like a typical Grey. The entity closed the door and Ed became fully aware of his surroundings. His arms were tingly and he was frightened and hyperventilating.

He realized that it was late and found that he was no longer on the road he was travelling on. He attempted to identify his location, when he saw a sign indicating that 1-75 and Lake City are ahead. Ed said emphatically, "I didn't drive here." He and Denise discussed their missing time and were anxious to go back to the field to check for the unusual objects they had observed only a moment before. When they arrived, the objects were no longer in the field. Ed was struck by the beauty of his dive that day, but felt unusually tired. I asked him if he discussed his missing time event with anyone that day other than Denise, and he replied, "I never told anybody about it. I never told anybody about it."

Ed later wrote to me:

The thing that struck me as being very strange is the alien's color. The eyes especially, even though they were the traditional shape and size seen in many drawings, this alien had eyes about three shades LIGHTER than the body color. (NOT BLACK) Also, there was no mouth or nose features. It was looking right at me when it put Denise in the seat. The features were very smooth like it was in some form of body suit. Its color was light green gray, the eyes light gray with no green. This is against all the mental images of what I would think an alien looks like.

Denise was anxious to discover the answers to questions she had pertaining to this mysterious event. We planned an additional hypnosis session to clear up any questions we still had. She easily slipped into hypnosis, and I asked Denise to return to the date in question. She

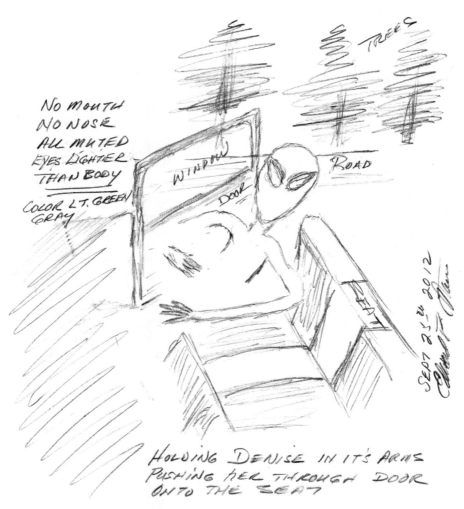

Ed's sketch of the alien placing Denise into the truck.

confirmed Ed's account of having breakfast at Nell's and returning to the motel for their gear. I asked her to move ahead a few minutes.

Kathleen: Your truck is loaded up now and you're heading north to your dive spot. You're travelling along Route 129 and approaching the farm on the right side of the road. You can tell me when you see the farm.

Denise: There are objects behind the building. There's an empty...I don't...I saw them, and they weren't normal, and I started to look around. There was an empty space on the left-hand side of the road—just a clearing. I said, "Look at those," and I pointed across, and I don't think Ed saw them. I think that it was too late. I don't know what the purpose of the clearing was or if there was anything beyond that. I can't place the clearing...if it was before the building or after. But that's the last thing I remember. Then we were...because I looked across at Ed and he was frozen to the steering wheel. [There is a long pause, and Denise takes several deep breaths.] And I was taken.

K: How were you taken? How did they do that?

D: A Grey took me—two.

K: Where were they when they took you?

D: I was sitting in the seat of the truck, and it felt like we were floating—like there was no gravity or something.

K: How did he take you?

D: He opened the door.

K: Okay.

D: And um...and the two arms, like the two arms on a forklift, went under me and pulled me out. But I didn't feel like I was sitting on anything.

K: Did you have your eyes open or closed?

D: Open.

K: Was it light or was it dark?

D: Light. Smoky. It was opaque. And very quickly I couldn't see the truck.

K: Do you know what happened to you or the truck—why you couldn't see it?

D: They sent it away...somewhere. It was almost like it was in a bubble that had no weight. It was almost like they just pushed it away.

K: Okay.

D: And then I saw the craft in front of me—a triangular craft.

K: Mhmm.

D: It was above what I thought was the road, but I think it was close to that open space where I saw the objects on the left.

K: Okay.

D: Oh...and they said they needed to borrow something from the power grid just for that small object. And um...I wasn't in there very long.

K: What happened when you were in there?

D: Oh...[sound of wonderment]. I think it had something to do with the thing in my head. They um...that being with the funny legs came and checked my head. But I don't know if that object was already there or not. I don't know. He did something to my head, and he said I shouldn't be afraid. For some reason I was very afraid that time. I was afraid I wasn't going to go back to Ed, and I was afraid I couldn't talk them into it. And he said, "There's no need for that." And I never opened my mouth.

K: Okay.

D: "There is no need for that. Do not dwell on it," he said. I wanted to know what he was fixing...what he was doing. And he said there is no need to fix anything. And it was brief little spurts that I'd receive that meant nothing to me. And I thought that I want to go back. Where is Ed? Is he all right? I saw him pushed away. He said, "It's all right. We've accomplished what we need to do." Then I was back, and I don't know how I got out of there. The next thing I remember I was on the side of the road, and I was sitting in the arms of this Grey. The door was open and he just slides me off his arms into the car seat.

K: Do you remember what the Grey looked like?

D: He was taller than the 4 feet. He was closer to...was 6 feet, maybe. He's very skinny, very thin and he can turn his head in a greater rotation of the neck. But yet, [there were] no joints that I could see. It seemed that when he needed to move, everything moved. He was almost like a Gumby. I remember how he opened the car door. It just opened or maybe it was left open. I don't know. I heard him make a crunching sound...like leaves crunching under his feet.

K: Can you see what color he is?

D: Kind of a bluish, grayish, greenish blue. Kind of odd.

K: Can you see his eyes?

D: It didn't seem like he had the unfeeling presence of a regular Grey when he looked at you, but I'm not sure. He had the eyes of a Grey but maybe not quite as large. I was very close to them... very close. I almost personally wanted to put a little tiny bit of a frame around it, so that told me he might have been wearing a protective suit. I'm not sure.

K: Take a look at his eyes. You can remember everything. What color were his eyes?

D: They were not black. They were kind of iridescent. I don't see any pupil really. It was kind of pale green...pale gray-green.

K: Were they shiny or opaque or somewhere in between?

D: I want to say somewhere in between, but I was so close that it almost looked to me like they had jillions of little dots in them. Millions and millions and millions...almost like they wanted to sparkle but they didn't.

K: Okay. You can go on. What happens next?

D: He stepped back, and I don't remember the car door closing. It just all of a sudden was closed, and it was almost like a bubble popping—a bubble filled with smoke. And we were driving, and I looked, at Ed and I was confused. I felt a combination of fear and yet I was put back—all of those emotions. And one of us said, "Where are we? What just happened?" or "It happened again"—something like that. And we have to figure where we are. We're not going in the right direction, and we have to find out. I was looking for street signs.

K: Did you find out where you were?

D: Yes, and I feel it now. I did not remember this until right now. I had a headache that was just nagging. It was like someone had taken a strip of something and put it across my head and tightened it down. And I was so confused. And every time I tried to figure out the whole set of circumstances and put them in some kind of order, it would tighten down on me. I feel it now.

K: You don't have to feel it now. You can relax.

D: It went across my forehead to my cheekbones to just above my ears.

K: You can go on. What happens next?

D: I hear Ed saying, "This is crazy. This doesn't make any sense." I said, "We know what happened. We don't have to try to figure it out because we know what happened." We had a little discussion back and forth. And he was looking around trying to figure out how to get us back in the direction we needed to go in. It's funny, because I've drawn a complete blank and I can't see around me.

K: It will become very, very clear now. You'll become very, very focused. You'll see it now. You'll see that point where you discover where you are.

D: I remember saying "Is this Florida? We need some sort of sign." For some reason, we were afraid to stop and ask somebody. [Something is troubling Denise, and she firmly says "Stop it".] I keep seeing this huge, huge face. This has never happened before. I don't know if it's a Grey or what it is. It's right in front of me every time I attempt to see.

K: You can let the Grey face go. It will have no impact upon you now.

D: I'd say it's Lake City. I think that's where we were.

K: Where is that?

D: I think its Lake City. I think it is. It's not super clear but I can't see anything else.

K: How did you discover that you thought you were in Lake City?

D: Ed discovered it.

K: Ed discovered it?

D: Mhmm.

K: Do you know how he discovered it?

D: We knew that area, and I think he mentioned, I believe first a landmark, but I'm not positive. A landmark...a place we had been...or possibly even a highway. I'm not sure. But he knew it. I didn't.

K: Okay. You can just forget about that now. Let it go. So now Ed has discovered that you are in Lake City. He knew it but you didn't. What did you do next?

D: He is going to turn us around and go back to Branford.

K: Did he do that?

D: Yes.

K: What did you do when you arrived back in Branford?

D: We were driving and talking about what happened. I was concerned because of the lateness and how much time it was taking. He was always very military back then.

K: So everything was on schedule?

D: Yes, very much so. And now it wasn't.

K: How much later was it than you anticipated?

D: I think at least 35–40 minutes...somewhere in there. Oh. [Pause.] I was looking at the sky, and I always did that for the time of day and getting an idea. You know—the sun coming up and the sun going down. I think we were going to go diving.

K: That's correct. You were going to go diving.

D: That whole weekend was Little River diving. 1-2-3...we just kept diving in the same spot, because I loved it so much.

K: Let's think about you being back on Highway 129, and you're heading toward Little River, and you're approaching the farm where you saw the odd-shaped structures in the field and behind the barn. Do you notice anything when you go by the barn?

D: Yes, those objects.

K: Are they still there?

D: No.

K: They're not there?

D: No. But I feel like whatever they were doing to my head the first time was completed. [She is referring to the previous night when she drove to a remote area off SR 247.]

Ed and Denise's separate hypnosis sessions have produced nearly identical information. The missing-time event occurred on Sunday morning, October 20, 1991, immediately after they observed strange, triangular-shaped objects in a field and behind a barn on CR 129 in Branford, Florida. Suddenly, they found themselves in Lake City and discovered that 30 to 40 minutes of their day had simply disappeared. Both recalled that Denise was lifted into the truck by a tall green-grey entity. Denise fills in the details about her time on the craft, which seems to have been for a simple maintenance checkup. They drove back to Branford and by the farm where they had observed the strange triangles, but the objects were no longer there. They arrived at Little River at 11 a.m. feeling mystified.

Now that the Stoner's missing-time events had gained some clarity and we were moving toward a resolution, I became curious about Denise's earlier involvement with extraterrestrial visitors. My research clearly indicates that the majority of abduction experiencers have been taken throughout their lives. I decided to inquire about her work with Dr. Romack and her earlier memories of possible alien contact.

6

Special Friends

In the 1980s, before the Stoners moved to Florida, Denise was able to step onto a path to recovering her forgotten memories, to fill in the blanks and recall events that had been long lost to her. She had responded to an advertisement in the Denver newspaper soliciting volunteers for an experimental study using hypnosis. The study was directed by Dr. Robert Romack and was designed to alleviate symptoms in chronic pain sufferers. He was developing a new hypnosis technique—a non-traditional medical treatment as an alternative to drug therapy. Denise had undergone abdominal surgery that left her with persistent pain and was interested in using alternative therapy for symptom relief. Dr. Romack enrolled Denise in his study after she demonstrated that she was an excellent hypnotic subject. She could relax enough to focus upon his voice and accept his suggestions. Additionally, she was able to reach a deep trance level of hypnosis.

After they became familiar with one another, Denise mentioned her UFO sighting and missing time event south of Jefferson, Colorado, to Dr. Romack. It was then that she discovered they had a mutual interest in UFO abduction experiences. They were both searching for answers to the alien abduction mystery, and she had partial conscious and continuous recall of personal experiences that were troubling her. He offered to hypnotize Denise to enhance her memory and remove any blocks that might be standing in her way. During the next several weeks, they began to learn some of Denise's suppressed memories.[1] Then new ones arose that were somehow related to her conscious memories.

I asked her to search her memory for possible youthful visitations with extraterrestrials. A few days later, I received the following passage:

> During the week of February 19, 1951 my mother was in the hospital giving birth to a new addition to the family—a baby girl—and my father was there visiting. My grandmother was working at the department store. I was 2 1/2 and being cared for by my grandfather.
>
> My grandfather was very close to me, his first grandchild, and he had cooked dinner for the two of us while I entertained myself. There was a small room with a sofa and table off the main living room where a play pen would go when my baby sister came home. I was standing on the sofa looking out a window directly behind the sofa. The curtains were tied back on each side, so just the blinds were covering the window. These blinds were open, leaving a clear view of the empty corner lot across the street and the telephone lines that stretched above it. The sky was dark with only a few of the brighter stars showing. No moon was visible, but the lot had a dim glow due to the lights emanating from the windows of other homes on either side of it.
>
> I did not miss my mother terribly that night, because grandfather and I had a very special relationship. Although I was very young, I knew he would be in soon to take me upstairs to bed. I thought warmly about how he always allowed me to select the bedtime story of my choice.
>
> As I peered out the window into the night sky, I noticed that not even a cloud was drifting by. Grandpa often sat outside with me playing a game of "find the animal shapes in the clouds." It was a pleasurable imagination exercise for my young mind. You couldn't do that on this night though, because the sky was crystal clear. Suddenly there appeared a huge yellow upright egg-shaped object in the sky outside the window. It hadn't been there a moment before. I had never seen an egg that big. It was

so bright, and there were beams of light coming off the egg. My young mind knew it wasn't the moon and decided surely it must be Humpty Dumpty. Perhaps my Grandpa had put him up in the sky for me to watch while he washed the dishes.

After a few minutes, my grandfather came into the room. He had a dishtowel draped over his right arm and just stood quietly observing me. I turned away from the window and asked, "Grandpa, why did they put Humpty Dumpty up in the sky?" I pointed through the blinds at the object still hovering just above the power lines. It was at least three times brighter than the full moon and many times larger. I carefully watched my grandfather's face and listened for his explanation. He peered through the blinds out the window. His face immediately registered fear, but a moment later returned to neutral.

Reflecting back on this moment as an adult, I realized that he had done this for my sake, so I wouldn't notice his discomfort. He reached past me and closed the blinds, blocking out the mysterious egg-shaped light. As if nothing unusual had occurred, he told me it was time to take a bath so I could get ready for bed. I never forgot how swiftly he had removed me from the scene.

Grandpa took my hand and helped me as I jumped from the sofa and continued to hold me as I climbed the stairs to the bath. Following a warm bath, he led me to my bedroom. The room was small—only large enough to hold a single bed, a dresser, and the baby crib that would soon belong to my new sister. Nursery rhyme figures in pale pastel colors graced my walls creating a cheery mood. He read my favorite story, and gave me a good night kiss. I was tucked in to my bed feeling secure and comfortable.

My grandfather went back downstairs and left me to fall asleep. I was lying still—thinking about the bright egg in the sky, when suddenly a small, dark figure appeared as if it walked out of the wallpaper. This little creature had on a hooded robe similar to a monk's attire. The sleeves were long so just the tips of his fingers showed at the ends of the dark fabric. He was carrying some sort of light or instrument with a light on the end. Instinctively, I knew this figure was a male. I felt more fascinated than afraid. He approached my bed and although his face was not clear under the hood with many folds, I somehow "heard" him say he was taking me with him for a ride, and not to worry.

I automatically sat up and stood on the floor, which felt cold on my bare feet. This small figure was not much taller than I was. He started towards the upper hallway and gestured for me to follow. I thought he might be showing me a trick by floating rather than walking. Just as we reached the top of the stairs, the figure turned towards the wall, reached for my hand, and then looked into my face. His eyes were huge and dark. I knew we were going to pass through the wall to get to the playground he promised to take me to.

This experience happened again and again in my young life. My parents believed I had an imaginary playmate, as many children do for a time in their early years before they've reached the milestone when they are able to separate fantasy from reality. Over and over again, they asked me what he looked like and what his name was. Thinking that I had a particularly vivid imagination, they just laughed at my fantastic stories and enjoyed each one.

Then one night, I awoke to find my baby sister missing from her crib. I went sneaking down the hall and peeked into my parent's room. But my sister was not there and my parents were in bed sound asleep. Where could my sister be? I wondered. She couldn't walk far without support.

A year passed, and my mother discovered her small daughter was missing from her crib. She worried because she assumed she was climbing out and sneaking downstairs in the middle of the night, where she could get hurt. In an effort to keep the young explorer penned in, my dad devised a plan. Soon he came home with tall pieces of plywood to build the sides of the crib up within feet of the ceiling. But his attempt to keep my sister out of harm's way would prove fruitless.

I knew this wouldn't do any good at all, because I had witnessed the small figure in his robe taking my sister with him during the night and bringing her back sometime later. This little man knew so many tricks, like walking right through the wall with no doors. He floated my sister right over the top of the foot of the crib while she was "sleeping" and back in when he brought her back. My sister did not appear to be hurt, so I never said anything about her "imaginary" friend taking her. I just listened and watched until it was my turn to go with the little man once again.

Why did I dream of being taken from my bed? Who can explain how I ended up on a street in my bare feet and pajamas running towards home but not quite making it? I wondered if I was dreaming at times, when I thought I was being taken from my bed to a place I was not familiar with. There was nothing to compare it to in my everyday world. How could I explain the little entities near my bed that had come to take me with them somewhere? What occurred in these strange surroundings prior to my return, I didn't know, except I became more fearful when attempting to force the memories to the surface? I soon realized that my memories were real.

One night I found myself in the park near my home. Looking behind me, I could see a tall skinny man, almost skeletal, with a huge head. He had big eyes that were very dark. His legs were spindly and not quite touching the sidewalk. His arms were long and thin. One arm had some sort of tool attached to it that looked like an old oil can. It had a long narrow tube on the end that dripped some sort of thick liquid that landed on the ground a drop at a time. This object on his arm made a "CLOCK CLOCK, CLOCK CLOCK" sound as the drops of liquid fell from the end. As I ran, the arm appeared to grow longer and came precariously close to overtaking me.

I had to get home. I knew I had been somewhere—taken from the security of my bedroom to a strange room that I could not escape from. My feet were wet and cold, and the legs of my pajamas were damp. I had awoken in the park without explanation, and was informed by someone that he could not return me to my bed. Who was he? I did not know. All I realized at that moment was the fact that "oil can man" was chasing me once again, and about to catch up with me.

Just as I reached the corner of my street, the arm reached the tip of my ear and a drop of the liquid trickled inside. I felt it enter the opening of my ear and continue down. The voice told me they would be able to keep track of me now as I grew up, and not to worry.

My next memory was of lying in bed, but not of waking from a dream. It seemed real. The sun was coming up. I sat up in bed. My covers were off and my feet were damp, along with the bottoms of my pajamas. I was afraid my mom would be angry, so I got up and put on my robe. No one would believe that a dream made my feet and pajama legs wet, so not wanting to cause problems for myself, I never spoke of this until I was in my 30s. The "dream" recurred over and over again throughout my grammar school years.

Though Denise believes that she had an almost idyllic childhood and a loving and supportive relationship with her parents, grandparents, and sister, she did have some fears and some phobias that seem to have been directly linked to her memories of nocturnal visitations. She states that she had an overriding fear of the dark and the entities that entered her bedroom from time to time. Her mother left a night light glowing near her bed and another illuminated the hallway that led to the security of her parent's bedroom. She and her younger sister shared a bedroom until Denise married and left home.

She realized, even as a young child, the she was experiencing something unusual, outside the realm of intervention by her family protectors. Somehow she knew that there was nothing she could do to prevent it. The strength of her family bond carried her though these nocturnal anxieties, and internally she knew that she had the fortitude to withstand her perceived situation. It wasn't until she was much older that she discussed her fears with her mother, and then it was only a brief exchange. Today she continues to temper her emotions and discusses her abduction experiences with only a few close friends.

During her childhood, Denise developed phobias that played out in repetitive behaviors. Nightly, she sat at the top of the stairs leading to her bedroom and etched a tall thin chair into the wallpaper. Today, this compulsive behavior reminds her of the movie *Close Encounters of the Third Kind*, in which the character played by Richard Dreyfuss character builds a tower out of mashed potatoes and ends up with half the soil from his yard in the living room. This behavior is commonly reported by abduction experiencers. It actually drives a person to continue searching for an answer without knowing why or what they are looking for, like a gigantic puzzle with many missing pieces.

Denise developed a phobia of places where there were many pipes, such as the control room in the basement of a ship or a hospital, where all the electrical systems, heating, cooling, duct work, etc., are grouped together. She felt that these pipes were going to reach out and capture her, hold her prisoner, take her away from her family forever. She never told her mother these fears. She avoided these situations or closed her eyes whenever she was forced to encounter them. She was also terrified of the miles of pipes outdoors that were fenced in and surrounded by hundreds of tiny lights at night—the ones owned by the power company.

She experienced anxiety whenever she accompanied her parents on rides to her great uncle's farm in New Hampshire. The roads that led to the farm were dotted with many clusters of these tiny lights and pipes. Denise had to close her eyes, fearing that if she opened them, "they" might come down to get her. She still cannot adequately explain this phobia in prosaic terms. The protracted nighttime drive through the woods was terrifying. She felt as if she was being followed even though she and her family were safely shielded inside the car. There was that haunting feeling in her head that "the long-armed man" always knew where she was.

She continuously sensed that she was being watched by some unknown source and would be taken against her will unannounced. It was a lot for a young mind to deal with. Denise never considered that others might be experiencing the same feelings. She thought that she was the only one. There was no one to talk to, and she did not want to worry her family.

It is unusual for an adult to so vividly recall memories of events that occurred at such a young age, but Denise maintains that they were sharp and clear above and beyond any others. This hyper memory could possibly have been retained as the result of a traumatic event she experienced. She had some odd physical illnesses as well. There were odd hive-like rashes on her arms and legs that the doctor could not relate to allergies.

She resisted going to sleep even with the lights on and had many strange dreams of medical procedures she knew nothing about. Her nights were long and filled with sleeplessness. Denise developed a fear of being alone, even for a little while. She wondered why, from time to time, she was observing small, gray, hooded figures around her. There were recurring dreams, plus some nosebleeds that her doctor attributed to growth spurts. Denise suspects that the insertion and extraction of implants were the real cause; not growth spurts.

As new revelations emerged, she became aware of experiences in her distant past that were somehow related to her recall of otherworldly visitations. Denise wrote:

What does it mean to be chased down the street by an unknown entity at twilight? Fear tracing every nerve without reason. That is what happened one evening, early, in California when I was walking home from a friend's home. There was no sound to alert me of the stranger following me, just the feeling in my mind that I should turn around and look back up the hill over my shoulder.

My home was at the very bottom of the hill which was also the end of the road. I was three or four houses away from my best friend's home. For some reason, I was hyper vigilant, aware of everything around me. I noticed that the sounds of the summer insects had silenced. None of the neighborhood cats were wandering about as usual. I turned to see a tall man—taller than usual—his stride moving him along towards me faster than it should without running. He was swinging his arms far out in front of him—arms that were unusually thin and too long. The whole picture was wrong. Who did he remind me of?

A series of memories fired in my brain. A young girl running down the street away from a monster of a man with a device in his hand shaped like an oil can clicking, dropping a substance on me. This couldn't be happening to me again. This person was going to overtake me and then what? I was a teenager now, not a child going back to my bed. I felt he would take me right off the street, against my will at dusk. Where were all the home owners? The folks who usually spent these pleasant evenings outdoors walking or visiting before going in for the evening? There was not a sound.

I picked up my pace and began to run, thinking I would dash to my best friend's home—hoping they were home—knowing I would be safe, and could probably just open the door and walk in without knocking. He was gaining speed, only a few feet from me now, his long ugly arms reaching for me already. His face could be seen clearly at this point. Those eyes and head absent of hair—pale flesh that was not the right color—this made no sense. I was hoping this was a costume of some kind and a joke was being played on me, but the odd feeling in my brain told me it wasn't the case.

I turned onto the gravel path leading to the front door, and twisted the door handle while banging hard on the door with the other hand. I turned to look over my shoulder to see the "man" run off to the side of the house and disappear into the back yard. My friend's dad answered the door and saw the immediate fear on my face. He stepped aside to allow me to enter. I was talking so fast he could not understand what I was saying, but did hear me say I wanted him to call the police. He was the father of six children and knew me really well, so did not question my request. He called out to all the other children who were home and asked them to move to the family room to sit together until the police arrived.

My best friend was there, along with two younger brothers. We sat together on a long sofa, all being very quiet. I did not describe what I knew but just explained there was a man chasing me. I felt foolish saying any more than that and thought I would not be believed should I describe the situation any further.

Minutes went by. All was quiet. My eyes were drawn to the sliding glass doors along the wall at right angles to the sofa I was sitting on. There was no light on and the backyards in this neighborhood were fairly large, filled with almond trees and California foliage of all kinds.

Soon there was a knock on the door. My friend and I looked up to see her dad go to the door and open it, allowing a police officer to enter. Although we girls were in our sophomore year of high school, we thought this policeman was very young. He asked to speak to me and walked through to the family room where all the kids were sitting. He interviewed me regarding the man who chased me. I felt I would not be believed should I say he was taller than normal, had arms that were odd, a gait that could not be easily described, and he could out run me by simply speeding up his walk, and seemed to be taking overly giant strides. I thought about the possibility that his feet were not touching the ground, leaving an inch between the soles of his feet and surface of the road. But no! I couldn't say this to the police or they would laugh and accuse me of making a false report.

So, instead I simply said I had been chased down the road by a tall man who had his arms out in an attempt to grab me. I didn't know him and I felt threatened. Having said this, the policeman exited via the front door and proceeded to the left side of the house heading to the backyard. The kids sitting on the sofa were watching through the sliding glass door and saw no one while this was going on.

I went back to sit on the sofa. We were all waiting for the policeman to come back to say he had caught the culprit, so all would feel safe. Suddenly, we could see the policeman's flashlight from far in the back left portion of the yard near the fence. It flickered on and off as he searched the area.

In the center of the yard was a huge trampoline everyone enjoyed jumping on several times a week. The front end of this could be seen faintly through the glass door. Suddenly, a shadow crossed in front of the trampoline blurring the shape of it. I and my friend noticed right away. We told everyone to look, to try to locate the flashlight. It was still shining in the back left corner of the yard.

Without warning, the shadow moved rapidly from the grassy area to the glass. There stood the creepy "man" in all his odd glory. He was almost pressed against the glass door so everyone could get a look. No one made a sound. Here was a thing that didn't look quite human. The top of his head disappeared above the frame of the door, making him at least 8 feet tall. Only the lower face could be seen. The inside light reflected on the gray-blue skin tone, revealing wrinkles where they didn't belong, and large eyes staring in at the group on the sofa. I noticed that only the head moved; not the eyes themselves, as if they were seeking me out. His eyes locked with mine. I attempted to look away but could not. I turned to see the other children sitting stock-still, unaware now of anything around them—not responding—not reacting to what they were seeing.

This creature was standing with those long arms; so long they were past his knees, and four fingers with arthritic-looking knuckles and a body that was too thin. Anorexic would be a good word to describe the being's allover appearance. There was some sort of "outfit" or uniform but I could not really describe it—only that it was the same color of this creature's skin.

I felt compelled to stand up and move toward the glass doors, open them, and step outside. My friend's dad was not in the room. I wasn't aware exactly where he was. I began to rise from the sofa in slow motion, my eyes locked with this tall man. I knew him from somewhere, and even though fear rang through my every nerve, I had no doubt I would move outside, as that was not something I had control over. My mind was foggy, my memory not clear, so I could not recall where I had seen this man before.

Just as I was about to open the slider, the front door burst open. There stood the young policeman, his eyes as big as dinner plates. He quickly slammed the door behind him as if the devil was chasing him down. My friend's dad came down the hall to the left where the bedrooms were to see what the noise was. He was a highly intelligent, scientific man who did not get overly excited about much of anything. He was very observant and could see there was fear on this policeman's face.

"What has happened here?" he asked. "Did you catch our bad guy?" The reply we all received was a total surprise. The cop didn't speak for a moment as if gathering his thoughts. He looked up at the small group gathered just inside the front door. He said, "My statement to you will be that I have only one flashlight, and I am not going out into that back yard again by myself. I can't call back up, because I don't believe I could explain the reason why I would require it. I am leaving now, so let's hope what is going on back there has gone and won't return."

I now began to get excited, wanting this thing to be captured. I raised my voice and in no uncertain terms told the cop to get back outside where he would find the "bad guy" as he had been standing at the back door looking in at us the whole time this policeman was out there searching for him.

This policeman opened the door and although he didn't run, moved as fast as he could down the walk, jumped into his cruiser and took off down the street. At the time this twisty, turny street was not well lit and was quite hilly. As soon as the police cruiser crested the top of the hill, he was out of sight.

We, the public, expect to be protected by the deputies sent to us to enforce the law. Certainly criminals escape and get away with no harm done only to commit another crime on another day when they do get captured. Somehow everyone in the room knew there was something different about this night. I and my friend began to realize the man at the door was not just a person wearing a costume.

My friend's dad stepped outside and watched while I ran down the street to my own home turning into my driveway at the bottom of the hill. I entered my house slightly out of breath and shut the door behind me. I did not lock the door, as somehow I knew it would not keep out this intruder who wanted to invade my teenage years as he had my younger ones. No one in the neighborhood locked their doors from dawn to dusk. It was a crime-free time of life, especially in this upper middle-class subdivision.

Would I tell my parents? Yes, I could talk to my mom. I could describe what happened in exact detail. My mom would believe me and not doubt what I said. There would not be many comments, but no doubt. My mother was fearful, but perhaps did not want to add any further uncertainty to an already unexplainable situation. So, she listened and said it made her feel creepy and unsettled. But what else could she do?

Surprisingly enough, nothing else happened to me during my high school years. Things were relatively easy. As I headed towards graduation, I had met the love of my life. The summer after my junior year I became a war bride and completed high school while my husband fought in Vietnam. He returned home safely the September after I graduated. We soon left California to begin our life together on the opposite coast on a military base.

A Lifetime of Abductions

Denise's next conscious memory of extraterrestrial contact came during Ed's brief stint at Colorado State University in Gunnison, Colorado. It was late afternoon, and Ed was seated on the balcony of their apartment building. The road to his right led to a sparsely inhabited hamlet high in the Rockies that today is a popular ski resort. For most of the year, it had only one way in and one way out, but during the short summer months, you could access it over a high unpaved mountain pass. There were foothills in front of him, across the field that swept to the right and began again on the other side of the road.

A sense of urgency filled Ed's voice as he called to Denise, "Come out here now!" She complied with his directive and soon was standing on the balcony peering at an aerial craft that in every respect seemed unconventional. Just over the top of the hill was a large, brushed gold disk hovering above the ridge. It was close—only a few hundred yards away. The late afternoon sun was reflecting off the metallic surface of the object. However, you could see round, porthole-shaped windows around the center. Ed had been a bit of a skeptic when it came to things like this, but Denise always thought there were strange things in life and one had to be open-minded. She was fascinated, although she felt an odd sense that this was somehow familiar. She just couldn't formulate a specific memory.

They watched as this craft hovered, then swept up and down the top of the hill. It dipped and swerved as if putting on a show to demonstrate

Denise on a mountain excursion in Colorado.
Credit: Ed Stoner.

its ability to maneuver in a way that most people had never seen before. This craft could turn on a dime. It remained level when making a 90 degree turn. It moved upward in a second and descended vertically with ease.

The two of them looked down and noticed that other young adults were returning from their classes. Denise shouted down to them and asked them to look up at the hill. The most perplexing reaction came from these students. The general response was "Oh, that thing? We see those all the time. It will fly away in a minute." It was as if they were not cognizant of the fact that this object was unconventional. Its unusual appearance and flight pattern meant nothing to them.

Denise felt like running down the steps to ask what in the world was wrong with them to cause such an unconcerned reaction. But something stopped her—she knew instinctively not to do that. What they needed to do was complete their packing and leave town as fast as possible—before the eerie visitors from her childhood reentered her life.

Intrusive memories of the "oil can man" and the diminutive gray figures pierced Denise's consciousness. She didn't want to revisit the troubling recollections from her childhood and felt a sense of urgency that she just had to get out of there—and fast. She, once again, began to feel the familiar odd sense that something from the past was watching her. She had forgotten her childhood anxiety about the "oil can man" and what it meant. There were no dreams to remind her. She wondered who the strangers were that interceded in her life. What did they want? She felt she had something locked up in her memories that needed to be released. Dr. Romack was the only person who could help her to piece together the puzzle that begged to be completed. She looked to him for answers as to what would be the source of a buzzing tone that had repeatedly alerted her to the presence of swirling lights outside her bedroom window. The lights penetrated into her bedroom and expanded into small figures at the foot of her bed. They were about 3 to 4 feet tall with huge dark eyes, no apparent clothing, no noticeable mouth or nose, and long arms with four fingers.

Fear enveloped her. She attempted to sit up but was only able to raise her arms. "No!" She screamed. "Not now!" But it didn't bring an end to her experience. She knew they were coming whenever an odd feeling in her brain signaled their impending arrival. It felt like nothing else she was able to describe. She felt herself lift off the bed, only to be returned after time had passed. She was certain of one thing: she hadn't been sleeping.

Once, after what she thought was an abduction experience, she tested positive on a pregnancy test. She lived in horrific fear of pregnancy, due to a past illness and being told she could not carry a fetus to term ever again. Then sometime during the first trimester, she awoke to find she was no longer pregnant. The baby had simply disappeared. Her womb was empty of all signs, and there had been no bleeding—no sign of a spontaneous abortion.

The second time was different than the first. She was carrying a baby the same as before, but this time pain and cramping were coursing through her body. Despite her discomfort, she was determined to join her family and a friend on a picnic in the mountains. Her cramping had persisted throughout the day, and when they arrived at the picnic area, Denise felt an urgency to rush to the outhouse. She emerged feeling lightheaded, and somehow knew that she had lost the fetus that she had been carrying. Feeling fearful, she climbed the hill, moving slowly in the direction of her family. Continuing to approach, she reached the top of the small rise, and there standing by a picnic area, as if frozen in time, were her husband and friend. They did not seem to notice her approaching and were gazing upward at something hovering just above the tree line.

Denise recorded her memories as follows:

I stepped into the clearing to get a better view of what my family was looking at. At the same time, I knew from here on, the rest of the day would be different somehow. I felt compelled to move forward, driven by a force I had no control over. Fear riddled my very being. Weakness overcame me as I contemplated the implication of what had just occurred in the outhouse at the bottom of the hill. This couldn't be happening again, could it?

I felt a presence and looked toward the wooded area. My eyes met a "thing" lurking just behind the nearby tree…watching me…observing my moves…telling me what to do next. It was the old familiar presence that had been with me since childhood. He seemed old by Earth years. I sensed that I would be going with him for a short time again. I knew I must step into the clearing and move under the light beam that would soon reach the ground. It was an old, familiar ritual. He stepped out from behind the tree and drifted closer to my side, sending instructions as he approached.

What happened next? My mind was screaming! I was aware of a sea of strange faces, an odd room, table, equipment, huge eyes... a familiar being. I had suddenly discovered myself back at the picnic area to find my family beginning to move about as if nothing had happened. I asked Ed if he recalled seeing anything unusual or felt something was wrong with the whole day. Did he feel time had passed that we were not aware of or what happened during those hours? Ed had no idea that anything unusual had occurred but did realize it was now getting dark and decided we should leave the wooded area to drive home before the sun fully set and the temperature dropped down as night set in. I felt alone and afraid with this horrific image in my mind of something I alone had witnessed aboard some strange craft no one else had seen.

Now was the time to go to Dr. Romack for sure. This needed to be cleared up for my own peace of mind, whether anyone else believed me or not. I picked up the phone and dialed the kind doctor's number.

Dr. Romack was anxious to help me and made an appointment for the following afternoon. I was to see him after his last patient with no limit on our time together. I was used to Dr. Romack's methods—I had practiced them myself when I wanted to relax in stressful situations.

Only feeling a slight anxiety, I entered the doctor's office the next day. I was ready to see what happened on that mountain top and to begin exploring the various unusual experiences in my life that had left so many blank spaces in my memory, along with frightening conscious pieces and parts, and also those shared with other witnesses giving me a sense that something did happen to me over and over again.

I was on the familiar sofa, lying back, and ready to begin. The doctor was ready to begin. He comforted me and reassured me that no matter what we uncovered, he would not ridicule or attempt to convince me I was wrong in my thinking. Now to begin the regression... One word and I slipped easily into hypnosis. Dr. Romack now took me back to the mountain top and the day of the picnic.

Soon I was on the mountain top. There I stood watching the lights flash among the trees. Yellow, red, blue, moving lower and closer. Why can't my family see them? I am mesmerized by the lights so I am unaware of the figure standing just to my right behind the bush, observing my behavior and level of fear. I look up to see a beam of light moving toward the ground. This alone has me in an almost hypnotic state. It is a beautiful color—looks like it would be warm feeling and inviting. This light moves ever closer to the ground near where I am standing, my family still frozen like statues...eyes wide open...not blinking but showing no fear.

I know instinctively the next minute will open a whole new view of something I have been shown but not allowed to recall until now. This minute I realize there is a small entity standing behind the bush to my right. He is looking right at me and I know him...have known him for a long time...perhaps since childhood. Although I am afraid, I do not attempt to run as he approaches me.

Dr. Romack recognizes the tension in my body and suggests I remain calm—it is a memory and he will help me through it. The familiar entity now asks me to step into the blue light. I feel as if I will be ripped apart, my cells separating. I move upward toward an opening that seems to be floating in the air. I can't possibly fit inside this opening. Where is the entity? He is there in the light beside me. Within seconds, I feel myself being sucked into the opening, and all at once, find that I am now again whole and standing in a hallway of sorts.

This hallway appears to be curved and dark yet has a dim source of light with no observable bulb. An odd glow lights the interior. There are other smaller entities with huge eyes lining the hallway. I think "soldiers" but have no idea where that came from. They show no recognition of me as a person—no feelings—and make no movement. I figure if I made an attempt to run away, they would be there to stop me so I don't test the theory.

My guide "tells" me I should walk down the hall and enter a small room to the right. It is a fairly empty place with a metal table in the center of the room that seems to be all one piece, including the base that is smoothly blended with the floor. There is a small panel on the wall showing 3 or 4 buttons visible including a screen that is blank presently.[1] I am asked to climb onto the cold metal table. I am resistant to do so and am thinking they will do me great harm. How can I get away? I am still in pain after what happened to me that afternoon and I don't want to be touched.

Another taller entity appears in the room. He could be a doctor perhaps, but not any doctor I had ever seen before. So, where did I get that idea? He has those huge eyes, no real nose or mouth, no visible ears, and odd skin. He is, however, wearing some sort of uniform that is tight-fitting. I lie down, thinking this is out of my control and I want to be back with my family, back on the picnic that seemed so normal—not like this craziness, although in some odd way this was a regular part of my life.

My familiar entity tells me there has been an "accident" and that I lost something in the outhouse today. I am not to go back in there, but use another area should I need to use a restroom prior to leaving for home. These entities were going to have to do some repair work on me to see that this is prevented from occurring again. A tool or instrument is lowered from somewhere over my head. It slowly enters my stomach just above my naval. The pain is excruciating and I scream. My familiar guide comes to the head of the table and places his hand on my face. The pain ceases immediately. You will not feel the pain and you will not remember this once you leave here.

Now the problem is, Dr. Romack has brought everything to the forefront, and I recall all of the blank spaces left from that afternoon on the mountain top. That picnic was so much more than hot dogs on a grill. What an absolutely ridiculous thought. Am I hysterical? There were several beings in a craft—beings with huge eyes and odd bodies so unlike ours, but had the advantage of having power over my actions, getting me to do what they wanted. Whose baby did I lose and why could I not see what it looked like? Or did I see what was in that outhouse and just could not bring myself to consider the possibilities. What happened to me in the blue light?

I was returned to my family that afternoon. I had no idea what the process was because that memory would not come back during hypnosis. I just found myself back on the ground standing next to the picnic table. My husband suddenly turned and spoke to me as if nothing happened and all was back to normal. He had no idea anything had gone terribly wrong a few minutes before and had a difficult time listening to me tell him what had gone on. He had to believe me when he looked at his watch, and then looked at the sky to see the sun was setting, and realized time was lost. We had arrived with plenty of time to light the coals and cook lunch. Now we would be eating in the dark. Where did the time go? I knew the answer to that now.

Denise soon learned that once she began the process of recovering lost memories others come to the forefront, without hypnosis.[2] She had full conscious recall of the following event:

One night, rotating lights appeared outside my bedroom window shortly after I had closed my eyes to go to sleep. The house was quiet...not a sound from my daughter or husband. I hoped I could get some rest as I was not particularly ready for sleep but knew I had to be up early. The lights were extremely bright, enough that I could tell they were there through my closed eyelids. I opened one lid and peered over at the windows to see the colored lights flash between the splits in the blinds. What was going on? The yellow lights were now in the bedroom floating around the bed.

This isn't normal. Before I could form another thought, there at the foot of my bed, a shadowy form took shape. I stared through the dark room, squinting to see what the dark form could be. A small, gray entity was standing there looking at me. This form had huge dark eyes that wrapped around an odd-shaped forehead. The eyes seemed to speak to me somehow. There was a voice in my head telling me to pay attention, concentrate, get up and follow "them" outside.

I sat on the edge of the bed, and then as if under remote control, I stood and stiffly moved forward toward the door entering the hallway, continuing down to the living room and front door. There were now at least 3 beings waiting to take me outside. Waiting a few feet past the front door, hovering over the quiet street, was a craft. Fear coursed through my body and brain.

A beam of light hit the street, and a familiar figure stepped out of the shadows, moving to my side. Somehow he conveyed to me that I should step into the light's beam. I knew I had to enter the light and proceed as directed. The rest is a blur until...I felt every nerve spark with pain. Strong emotions streamed through my very being.

I was standing in a strange room filled with clear containers in all sizes lining the wall on one side beginning with individual life-size, tube-shaped structures coming toward me in rows growing smaller until what they held were.... I closed my eyes tightly and clenched my fists wishing against all odds that this scene would disappear when I again opened my eyes. Was this a dream or some kind of trick my mind was playing?

The familiar being indicated somehow I should open my eyes and look into the containers and walk along the isles with him. I obeyed, as there seemed to be no other choice. There, floating within these clear objects, were beings. Some were almost the size of human newborns. They appeared to be somewhat human in shape with differences in skin color, number of fingers and size of eyes, with little or no hair.[3]

We next moved to smaller but similar vials. Then, in amazement, I knew as I approached the vial closest to me—this was the baby I had somehow "lost" the first time, the missing pregnancy. I felt a connection to the being within the artificial womb. There was a quickening, a sudden stirring in the fluid. I dropped my eyes downward just in time to see the eyes flicker, then open slightly. Here were huge, dark vessels containing all the knowledge of where they came from...at least it seemed that way. I searched their depths for recognition—a contact between two totally different beings. I knew in my heart that this was my child, no matter where or how it was conceived. I also knew I would probably never see it again. It would be ripped from my presence. More truthfully, I would be taken from this place. What was happening to me? How would I go on with a so called normal life knowing in my mind, this other place or time existed? Who in the world would ever believe this insanity?

Once again, there is only one person I can go to and that is Dr. Romack. This time a conscious memory is flooding my thoughts. There is something I must tell him before I can continue to see if I am able to trust him with unbelievable mind-blowing information. Would he now tell me that I am crazy?

Prior to her next visit with Dr. Romack, there was an eyewitness event that gave confirmation to Denise's story. It came from the neighbor across the street, and she was forever grateful for this tiny testimony indicating the episode she had just experienced was not a dream. Denise was elated that this small substantiation lent so much probability to the truth factor of her nighttime trek.

There was a wonderful close-knit family across the street from Denise's home. The older woman, Paola, often took care of Denise's daughter, Dienna, so she and Ed could get away for an evening. Paola and her husband also cooked terrific Mexican dinners and took them to Denise's home to share together. Not long after Denise awoke with memories of her abduction event, Paola asked her what she was doing out in the middle of the road "the other night" in her pajamas. Denise asked, "What night was that?" Paola replied, "The night the bright light was going up into the sky, and you were coming out from underneath it." She woke her husband, and they returned to the front door in time to see Denise entering her front door.

Denise decided to disclose this new information to Dr. Romack prior to her next hypnosis session. He suggested she return to the night in question without distress or upset. She saw herself standing next to the small container where the tiny being floated in silence. She heard a sound to her left. There was an opening in the wall she hadn't noticed before and a person entering the room—a being that looked almost human in appearance. This was a female whose eyes were not as large as the other entities. Her body was more graceful and quite slender. The skin tone was slightly tanner in shade than the odd grayish look of the "soldiers" with the huge eyes. She had more of a mouth and nose and what may pass for small ears under thin blond hair. Holding her hand was another child looking much like her. Denise's escort indicated she should follow them in to another area of this place she had been taken to against her will. She was now bound by emotions stronger than any fear tempting her to run from these beings.

Denise wrote:

I entered a small room devoid of any furniture, panels, or other items on the wall. When asked to sit on the floor, I did so. No words were spoken by the child. I did not feel uncomfortable in the presence of these beings and began to form questions in my mind. Suddenly responses came to me in exchanges shared across the space somehow between the two of us—two adult species of humans, I supposed, who could share information about each other and how we each functioned. Where did that come from I wondered? I thought I "heard" that in order for either species to survive, changes had to be made and they were responsible for making those changes, as their planet was going to be the first one to lose its grip on life, and they would have to leave to search for another life source or planet that would suit them. So far we were the best combination or mixture of life structures that seemed to blend together to create a better functioning being.

I did not feel any connection with this child—not the bond I had with the being in the vial out in the other area. This was a life lesson of some sort and I had to sort it out. Why was I chosen? What did it mean? I was going to ask these things over and over again until something clicked—some reasoning came together within myself that made sense if only to me.

I was guided down the rounded hallway, and again the small soldiers were lined up like statues against the far wall. A tiny bit of fear crept in to my body. All of this was unfamiliar, no one believed in flying saucers; never mind what I had just experienced. I had so much to take in and accept inside myself. Suddenly I felt my feet touch the street, with no memory of how I reached the road in front of my home. I only knew I needed the familiar—my bed and my husband.

Personal accounts of alien abduction such as the ones presented in this chapter by Denise are perplexing. Some were brought to the forefront through hypnosis, but others are part of Denise's conscious, continuous recall. Some of these events are personal memories that she experienced as real, but cannot be substantiated by eyewitnesses. Although her memories are subjective, there is sometimes a morsel of confirmation that they might be real. This is the case in the story of an abduction where Denise saw a familiar face and possibly encountered "Jennie Henderson," whose story appears in the second section of this book.

One morning within the past several years, Denise awoke in her Florida home with vivid memories of finding herself on a huge, roughly triangular-shaped craft that she described as "thick in the middle and rounded on the ends with a slightly curved rear section." A long row of rectangular windows lined the front and a balcony slid out beyond the windows. She found herself in a dimly lit hallway among a cluster of people waiting to be taken into one of several rooms where the Grey aliens seemed to be carrying out a large-scale project. The fearful people were huddled together and the Greys seemed concerned that the project was not going well.

A woman with freckles and graying, copper-blonde, chin-length hair was standing several feet away from Denise in a different group.

She was wearing light-colored lounging pajamas and wanted no part of the ET's project. She clasped hands with a younger woman and attempted to flee. Denise did not know her fate, as she was quickly led away toward the rectangular windows.

She and several others were led to the balcony where she observed a mountainous region and a cluster of chalets below. The frigid wind was whipping against her face. The craft approached the jagged edge of a granite cliff, and she could see the forest below. She looked to her left and saw a woman wearing a cocktail dress with a sparkling scarf and beautiful brooch. The man next to her had a familiar appearance. He was dressed in a light gray jogging suit with black and white stripes on the arms of his jacket and pants. She could see a blue Nike symbol on his shoes, and he was not wearing socks. Everyone appeared nervous and frightened.

When the craft dipped at an angle above the treetops, the group was instructed to release the lightweight, charcoal, metallic cubes into the forest below. Their mission accomplished, they were led back inside. The balcony slid back into the craft and the windows came down over it. There was an urgency that something had not gone well. Denise awoke in her bed with icy cold, rosy cheeks, as if she'd been outside in the snow wondering if her dream had been real.

She later encountered the man wearing the jogging suit at a function and without revealing where she remembered seeing him, asked if he had clothing that matched her description. He answered in the affirmative. This gave Denise an additional morsel of confirmation that the event was real and not a dream.

As Denise related her story to me, it seemed like déjà vu. I checked my files and discovered that "Jennie," the abduction experiencer in the second half of this book, recalled an eerily similar event that she had experienced as a vivid dream. Jennie had awoken with information nearly identical to Denise's. Whether or not this was a dual dream, she might have been the woman with shoulder-length, copper-blonde hair that Denise observed attempting to flee. She was intercepted and led to a balcony, where a frigid breeze lashed her face. A woman that she didn't recognize, but who fit Denise's description, caught her eye. She was clothed in white and blue patterned pajamas with ruffles around the legs. I asked Denise if she owned a pair of pajamas that matched Jennie's detailed description and was astounded when she replied in the affirmative. This serendipitous event is mystifying to me and beyond the scope of what I had anticipated from two experiencers with whom I have worked. Either each woman had a nearly identical dream, or the experience was real.

● ● ● ● ● ● ● ● ● ● ● ● ●

8

An Evaluation
of the Evidence

Individuals, such as Denise, who claim to have participated in extraordinary experiences are often looked upon with skepticism. Is the person telling the truth? What is the content of his or her character? Is he or she emotionally stable? Does he or she have well-delineated boundaries between fantasy and reality? Were there witnesses? Is there evidence? Were there conscious, continuous memories? All of these things must be evaluated.

The best way to proceed, in my opinion, is to assess the evidence on its merits, much as a district attorney would be charged with the responsibility of determining whether or not there is sufficient evidence to prosecute a case. Statements constituting a deposition must be taken from each witness to determine whether or not there is sufficient evidence to go to trial. In Denise's case, she is the plaintiff and the alien abductors are the defendants. The question that begs an answer is, Has Denise been abducted from her natural environment by non-human entities at least one time?

The most solid evidence in Denise's case is the August 13, 1982, missing-time event in South Park Valley, Colorado. Denise and Ed have clear, conscious memories of descending Kenosha Pass and traveling through Jefferson. Denise recalled observing two rapidly approaching bright, yellow lights which she pointed out to Ed. He thought that she was pointing to a house under construction. Then suddenly and without warning, the car shifted off the highway. As if only a moment had passed, they found themselves, without explanation, at a distant location on Trout Creek Pass at the opposite end of the valley. Forty miles and three hours time had simply vanished. There is no acceptable prosaic explanation for this time lapse.

In addition to Denise and Ed's testimony, Denise's mother has sworn that they arrived hours later than anticipated. She, along with Denise's husband, has submitted signed statements as evidence. Denise and Ed experienced a strong emotional reaction to the missing-time event. Ed was hyperventilating, disoriented, and perplexed. Denise was stunned and shaken beyond words.

Their second major missing-time event is as perplexing as the first and induced the same emotional response as was experienced in the first major event. There is no rational reason for rejecting it out of hand, despite the fact that Ed and Denise are the only witnesses.

The Stoners are honest, grounded, hard-working individuals. By all accounts, they are credible people of excellent character. Neither has a history of substance abuse or psychiatric illness. Both were raised in supportive, loving households. Neither spouse is overly dependent upon the other. They have a harmonious relationship founded in mutual respect and consideration. There is no reason to believe their lost-time experience was fabricated or has a valid psychological explanation.

The Stoners are not seeking fame or fortune by coming forward with their story. They know it is more likely they will be subjected to a negative assessment by a few overzealous debunkers and ufologists with biased opinions against alien abduction reports. Any fame that comes from this disclosure will be tempered by mankind's propensity toward attacking the victim of an anomalous experience. Often, anyone who is perceived as different is an easy target for adult bullies, who may invent false information which distorts the public's perception of the truth. No witness has ever become wealthy by taking his or her abduction experience to the public. Little or no money is offered for television appearances, and books of this nature have a limited market. Ed and Denise Stoner are heroes who have come forward at this time, because they are retirees with little to lose, except their good reputations.

There is a movement afoot for abduction disclosure and thousands more are wrestling with the idea of revealing their identities.[1] It is a difficult decision for anyone to make, and all sides of the question must be assessed. The benefit of coming forward with this information lies in the support one can garner from those who have had similar experiences. Much healing can be accomplished, discussion can be initiated, and understanding can occur.

Although often accurate, when a hypnotized individual is pushed for information that doesn't exist in one's biographical memory, there is a propensity to fill in missing details from one's imagination.[2] For this reason, the information that Denise revealed in hypnosis comes with no guarantee that it is objectively real. It might be entirely accurate, but the possibility exists that it is not. For this reason, her detailed memories must be compared with little known information reported by numerous independent experiencers. The "Marden-Stoner Commonalities Among Abduction Experiencers" study supplied some of this detailed information.

Fifty self-identified experiencers participated in the Marden-Stoner study, along with a control group of 25. The 45 questions for the experiencer group were broken down into five categories: demographics, abduction memories, paranormal experiences, emotional responses, and physiological responses. Only 23 of the 45 questions yielded correlating results. The answers were compared to responses from a control group that denies having experienced alien abduction. Not all participants answered all questions. Some could not recall or did not know the answer. Fractions were rounded off. A statistical analysis of the responses revealed that the experiencer group shares a unique constellation of characteristics not found in the control group.[3] (See the complete report at *www.kathleen-marden.com.*) To ensure that Denise's memories were not influenced by the study, I withheld the final results from her until after her hypnosis sessions had terminated. She shares the following correlating characteristics with the self-identified abduction experiencers who participated in the study:

1. Denise and 64 percent (32 of 50) of the experiencers are women.

2. She and the majority of experiencers (37 of 47 that answered the question) believe that they have been taken repeatedly over a number of years or throughout their lifetime. Only 2 of the experiencer group reported one abduction only. 8 were not certain.

3. She and 25 of the 39 participants in the experiencer group believe they have been taken more than 10 times. (Eleven did not answer or were not certain.)

4. She and 18 of the 42 participants in the experiencer group that knew their approximate age when their first abduction occurred indicated that they were under age 5. 35 stated that they were under age 20, 7 were over 20, and 8 were not certain.

5. She and 32 of 42 experiencers that answered the question (76 percent) indicated that they were not alone when they were taken. Denise stated that her husband was with her when most of her abductions took place, either outside or when she was taken from her bed. He realized something out of the norm had occurred.

6. She had conscious recall for at least part of her abduction experiences, as did 88 percent (44 of 50) that answered the question. She also recalled it though dreams, like 56 percent of experiencers, and through hypnosis, like 36 percent of experiencers.

7. She and 67 percent (28 of 42) stated that they consciously recalled (not with hypnosis), the observation of an unconventional craft at less than 1,000 feet prior to an abduction experience.

8. She and 56 percent stated that they had conscious recall (not with hypnosis) of observing non-human entities immediately prior to an abduction while they were outside their home.

9. She and 43 percent stated that witnesses reported the observation of a UFO near their house, vehicle, tent, etc., prior to an abduction. On two occasions, neighbors witnessed lights

over Denise's house and in a green belt area near her home where she recalled being taken.

10. She and 58 percent of the experiencer group are aware of having been examined on an alien craft.

11. Following an abduction, she and 68 percent of the experiencer group reported malfunctions of electrical equipment such as lights, digital watches, computers, etc. 32 percent of the control group reported similar malfunctions.

12. She and 88 percent (43 of 49) of the experiencer group have witnessed paranormal activity in their homes, such as light orbs, objects that fly through the air, lights that turn off and on, doors opening and closing, etc. Of the 43 that answered in the affirmative, 22 stated that it began after their first abduction. 44 percent (11 of 25) of the non-experiencer group reported that they have witnessed paranormal activity in their homes, such as ghosts, shadow people, spirits, strange sounds, and variations in room temperature. Denise states that mail and jewelry inside her home was inexplicably missing, but later reappeared in an odd location. One piece of her jewelry has never resurfaced. Another lost item inexplicably reappeared in a conspicuous location at a much later date. She has also heard odd noises (not related to normal household sounds), and observed light orbs in her home.

13. She and 88 percent (44 of 50) of the experiencer group reported they have received telepathic messages from their ET visitors. Ninety-one percent (30 of 33) stated that these messages were related to an abduction experience. 32 percent of the non-experiencer group (8 of 25) reported telepathic communication.

14. She and 50 percent (25 of 50) stated that they have been given a gift of healing following an abduction experience. Denise stated that this occurred for a brief period of time, especially with animals.

15. She and 72 percent (36 of 50) stated that they are more sensitive or intuitive than they were prior to the abduction.

16. She and 79 percent of those who responded (26 of 33) stated that they developed new psychic abilities after an abduction experience. (Two experiencers stated "maybe" and 15 were not able to answer the question.)

17. On a daily basis, her mood is happy and/or without unusual highs or lows, as was the case for both the experiencer and control groups. (Experiencer group (50): 15 happy, 25 without unusual highs and lows, 7 sad and 8 with frequent mood swings. Non-experiencer group (25): 15 happy, 6 without unusual highs and lows, 0 sad, and 4 with frequent mood swings. Participants could check more than 1 response.)

18. As a child, her mood was happy and without unusual highs or lows, as was the case for the majority of participants in both groups. As a daily coping mechanism to deal with any fear or anxiety due to her abduction experience, she uses meditation, reading, writing, talking with friends, watching educational television shows, and keeping busy. (This is an open-ended question. Many stated that they found relief from meditation and an equal number found relief from talking with friends.)

19. Her emotional response to her abductions is consistent with that of other abduction experiencers' responses. She stated that she felt confused and disoriented. At times when she knew she had been taken, she felt anger knowing that her life was in the entities' hands and out of her control. She knew that they didn't have to return her to her natural environment if they did not wish to.

20. She and 74 percent (37 of 50) of the experiencer group have difficulty falling asleep. She and 71 percent (35 of 49) of the experiencer group have difficulty staying asleep. (The majority of those who are able to sleep through the night attribute it to healing or loss of fear through hypnotherapy.)

21. She and 83 percent (40 of 48) have awakened with unexplained marks on their bodies, such as burns, puncture wounds, bruises, and evidence of a bloody nose. Only 20 percent (5 of 25) of the control group reported awakening

with unexplained marks on their bodies. Denise stated that she found a fresh scoop mark wound on her leg and three triangle-shaped marks in a circle that she photographed. She also awoke while an entity was pushing a tool with a red hot object down her throat. Her tongue was burned and remained that way for three days.

22. She and 69 percent (22 of 32) of the female participants have experienced gynecological problems that they suspect are related to their abduction experiences. 33 percent (3 of 9) of the female control group reported experiencing gynecological problems.

23. She has been diagnosed (tentatively), as having chronic fatigue syndrome or reactivated mononucleosis; 38 percent (18 of 48) of the experiencer group has this diagnosis, although the prevalence among the general population is less than 1 percent for CFS. Two additional experiencers state that they have the symptoms but no formal diagnosis.

24. She and 62 percent (29 of 47) of the experiencer group crave excessive amounts of salt. Only 12 percent (3 of 25) of the control group reported this craving.

25. She and 53 percent (21 of 40) of the experiencer group believe that they can feel an alien implant in their body. Denise felt one near her knee, but it is now gone and has been replaced by a scoop mark (punch biopsy) type scar. I observed and manually examined a pea-size lump in her lower arm that moved upward to her shoulder over a 5 day period and then disappeared.

I asked Denise to evaluate the evidence in her case. She is a longtime UFO investigator and abduction researcher and was Florida MUFON's chief investigator when we met. For many years, she independently investigated her own experiences attempting to find her own truth. She wrote the following assessment of her case:

What evidence would I have to prove beyond the shadow of a doubt that I was abducted by an alien race from a place other than our own planet Earth? How do we as investigators gather that evidence and what do we look for as markers? From the very beginning, I have felt lucky because I have almost always had more than one witness, other than myself, involved somehow when I was "taken." Along with missing time, there have been crafts involved, entities sighted, and some sort of physical affect left over as a result of the abduction. On the other hand, none of this is an exact science and is something we are just scratching the surface on. Information gathering in a very careful manner is of utmost importance. Every attempt is made when accepting a possible abductee for study to make sure they do not know others we are working with or have shared stories, with the exception that we are dealing with a shared experience. Careful documentation is done, studied, compared with others, and filed for later reference.

I asked Denise what effect alien abduction has had upon her life. She replied:

Personally, I would have to say that after a lifetime of experiences, this has had a profound effect on many areas of my life as a whole. Once I reached the stage of my life where I was old enough to reproduce, my health was never what we'd call normal. Not only that, my illnesses were and are so unusual that I was informed that one is written up in a medical journal. I have copies of two MRIs taken of my brain. They show some abnormalities on the left side and my neurologist stated that the techs do not know what the tiny specks are. He said if pushed they would compare it to several diseases we recognize, but it is not written in concrete, and I do not test positive for any of them. I had unexplained nose bleeds as a child. I was told I had growing pains in my legs to explain the odd numbness that woke me up in the middle of the night. But I knew this was not an accurate diagnosis. Chronic fatigue syndrome is another debilitating disease common among abductees. It takes a doctor's diagnosis. My doctor has suggested that I might have this disease.

As a young woman and mother I certainly had some trauma following what appeared to be "missing" pregnancies followed by visits to crafts where I was shown fetuses in vessels that could have been mine. No more nighttime visits, I was taken during day light hours, knowing I would be taken and a sense that I had no choice in the matter, I was going to a craft and had no say in it at all. I lived with this for years, but in some way decided it was just a part of my life and had been for so long; perhaps others had this secret dual life also.

Among some "experiencers," there are surgical scars that appear fresh, suggesting that the person must have undergone an operation. These scars look laser clean and are not closed with sutures. They also have the ability to heal rapidly—within a day or two. Perfect circular wounds that resemble a biopsy are common. A small plug of skin and muscle has been removed, as if a small tool resembling an apple corer type device, only cleaner, lifted a sample from the person for scientific study or for some reason we are not aware of as yet. I have these scars.

I did not need a book to tell me what to believe or how to handle what I had gone through and was continuing to go through. This was a part of my existence. I was still here, still had the same beliefs, no one had taken them away, I would have to do that myself and choose that. The only difference was, if the visitors came, I had no control over their motivations and/or control over me. At the same time throughout my 64 years of these experiences, I have been returned to my home and family following each one, have learned so much about places I truly know exist, met beings who are so much more advanced than we are and may know at least some of the secrets of the Universe, and would not give any of it back if I could. This has perhaps given me a touch of wisdom I would not have regarding people and choices and living our lives to the fullest of our abilities and this has all meant a great deal to me. Looking at this as a whole, every bit means a lot and will continue to as I further my work in this arena.

As is the case in any alien abduction report, the investigator cannot affirm or deny the reality of the experience unless it is supported by unambiguous corroborating objective data. Denise has unequivocal circumstantial evidence that she and Ed experienced a 3-hour time lapse in Colorado. Two additional surviving witnesses (her mother and

Dienna) swear to the missing-time event. She and Ed have testified that they are aware of additional experiences.

Although her childhood memories of possible alien contact are interesting, they are a combination of consciously recalled events and recollections brought forth through hypnosis with Dr. Romack. Memory is fallible and information retrieved through hypnosis is not reliable. That said, it is important to note that Denise shares a commonality with the self-identified abduction experiencers who participated in our study; 56 percent of the study's experiencers reported that their first abduction occurred when they were less than 10 years old and 36 percent stated that they were less than 5. Denise believes that her first contact occurred at age 2 1/2.

Denise also shares commonalities with other abduction experiencers that are not widespread across the general population. One might argue that the answers to some questions on the "UFO Abduction Experiencer" questionnaire are well-known among abduction experiencers, and therefore might present a skewed, inaccurate result. For example, we inquired about the presence of a possible implant that can be detected through touch. Alien implants have been publicized by the media and were reported by 53 percent of the self-identified abduction experiencers who participated in our study. But the study asked numerous questions pertaining to information that is not generally recognized as being part of the alien abduction constellation of symptoms. Additionally, not all questions pertained to reported information specific to abduction experiencers. Every effort was made to avoid obtaining inaccurate or misleading results. At the inception of our study, Denise did not know what she had in common with other experiencers, except for information that had already been published. Her responses on the questionnaire are compelling and suggest that she has nearly all of the characteristics of an abduction experiencer.

An evaluation of the circumstantial evidence in Denise's case might lead a district attorney to prosecute the case. The evidence suggests that crimes have been committed against her. These include kidnapping, bodily injury, emotional harm, and illegal medical experimentation. But the perpetrator has not been arrested and the authorities are ignoring the witnesses. Authoritative declarations of impossibility have been offered by well-educated but uninformed individuals. As a result, we as a society have come no closer to the truth than we were 50 years ago. Prosaic explanations have been offered, but in order to accept them, one has to turn a blind eye to the evidence. Thus far, no one has offered a credible prosaic explanation for alien abduction, especially when the abductee is of sound mind, has conscious, continuous recall of the event, corroborating witnesses, and missing time that defies explanation.

A Day of Reckoning

January 16, 1988 had been a typical Saturday in the Henderson household. Jennie and her family had spent the night together, devouring a pepperoni pizza in front of the fieldstone fireplace at their rural New Hampshire home. A movie played on their VCR, as her youngsters, 10-year-old Sarah and 12-year-old Aiden, slumbered in front of a crackling fire with their 4-year-old boxer, Poppy.[1]

Growing tired, the two adults hastened the children to bed as soon as the movie ended. After a busy week, they were looking forward to a restful night. Sleep came quickly. But sometime during the night, Jennie was awoken by Poppy's piercing yelps. She invariably sounded a familiar warning whenever a guest approached the Henderson's rural farm home. Jennie had become accustomed to hearing it. Poppy was an affectionate dog and a loyal pet for Aiden and Sarah, but her protective nature caused her to go on alert whenever company stopped by. Jennie had attempted to train her to be less defensive, but Poppy relentlessly sounded a vicious warning and bared her canines with each approaching car. It was a major inconvenience when friends came to visit, but the Henderson home was isolated, on the outskirts of town, and Jennie was often home alone with the children, and several homes on their street had been burglarized. Poppy was good protection.

Early the next morning, as she lay upon her pillow, eyes cracked open, filled with unnerving thoughts, she focused upon the bright strands of morning light that penetrated the diaphanous curtains in her upstairs bedroom. January's crisp breeze puffed through the partially opened window, causing them to dance lightly, a frivolous distraction from the weight of her memories of the previous evening.

Her mind focused on Poppy's behavior in the dark loneliness of the previous evening. Jennie mulled over the wailing yelps that were ascending toward a feverish pitch, followed by a sudden wall of silence. It was as if Poppy's vocal cords had been severed in canine mid-sentence. There was no crescendo, no winding down, no ebb to the flow—only silence.

Whatever had caused Poppy to sound a ferocious alert during the night had apparently retreated from the area. There had been a family of coyotes spotted in the backwoods last fall during hunting season, and perhaps one had caught the scent of the chicken coop, sensing an easy predatory feast. But the shed was securely locked and impenetrable. There was no need to send Doug out into the frigid night air to investigate.

Jennie seemed to recall the rushing of footsteps and the rapid entry of someone into her bedroom. Had one of her children hastened to her bedside seeking her maternal reassurance? Perhaps Sarah had come down with another one of her night fevers? Or Aiden sought his mother's comforting touch after awakening from another recurring nightmare about strange symbols that he couldn't seem to get out of his head? "Too much pressure in that new math class," she thought.

But she couldn't remember rising to tend to the medical or emotional needs of her youngsters. What flashed across her mind was the memory of her husband's defensive stance at the bedroom door and a group of intruders who, with the precision of a well-drilled team of military officers, laid his limp, immobile body down on the bed. Seconds later, what seemed like more than one diminutive figure rounded the foot of the bed, hovering in silence. Her gaze met glistening cat-like eyes—those huge, fluid, penetrating, crazy eyes sent her heart racing and body quivering. A tingling numbness slid up her toes and gushed like a swollen creek toward her head. From deep within her belly came a low-pitched scream—don't! She was paralyzed. Her next memory was of waking up trembling, heart pounding in the morning light.

Jennie pondered her vague memories of nocturnal activity that had been so disquieting only hours before. Was it only the manifestation of a waking dream? Sleep paralysis? This was not her first frightening nocturnal interruption.

Jennie shifted her dreamy eyes to the spot where Doug had lain beside her. It was vacant and cool. She heard a wood fire crackling in the fireplace below and sniffed the cozy scent of maple that was wafting plumes of warm air into her bedroom. He had risen before her to read the Sunday paper and begin the morning preparations for breakfast and church.

The aching tension in Jennie's body could only be relieved, she thought, by the comforting stream of hot water from her pulsating shower head. It always seemed to do the trick when she awoke with stinging tightness in her muscles and tendons. Lumbering out of bed, she stepped into her bathrobe, pulled up the zipper, and headed for the bathroom, glimpsing crimson streaks upon the pillowcase where she had rested her head. Her eyes opened wide, and her mouth dropped in shock and disbelief. Searching for a prosaic explanation she reasoned that the dry winter air caused her to have a nosebleed.

Entering the bathroom, Jennie splashed cool water on her milky, freckled complexion and stared at the red capillaries running like roadmaps around the crystal emerald irises of her stinging eyes. Tears welled up, without sadness, and released trails of burning fluid down her cheeks, leaving paths trailing to her chin.

She reached for the light switch, but her fingers drew an electrically charged spark, and the light bulb blew out with a pop. Lucky for her, Doug had installed a skylight when he replaced the roof last year. It let in just enough morning light to illuminate her shower. It would do in a pinch until she could change the bulb. She stepped into the warm stream of water and let it run through her wavy copper-gold hair, over her cheeks, and down the curves of her back. Suddenly, her back screamed from the pain of weeping, raw flesh, and she quickly adjusted the faucet to a cool flow. In haste, she pumped a dollop of shampoo into her left hand and quickly rubbed her palms together before distributing it through her saturated strands. Another wave of dread passed through her when she realized that her shoulder-length hair had taken on the texture of rough, sunburned corn silk.

Bending toward the bottle of conditioner Jennie's eyes glanced at a wad of tangled hair bobbing in the rising water on the tub's floor. Fox-colored tangles streaked the surface and filled the drain clogging the flow of water. Shocked, she gasped, "Oh my God! It happened again." She straightened her ankle and pointed the toes on her right foot to drag the tangled mat from the drain as she pumped gobs of conditioner into her left hand. Then, she broke down into body-wracking sobs.

After rinsing her hair, Jennie cut the flow of water and reached for the tangled mass of copper-gold strands, scooping it from the tub. With a taut flick of her wrist, she deposited it into the woven waste-basket that one of her students had made for her the previous school year. She stood rigid, determined to regain her composure in front of her full-length antique pine mirror. As she examined her naked form, she studied the throbbing red ribbons of oozing flesh that trailed from the tops of her shoulders toward the gently sloping curve of her but-tocks. Searching her medicine cabinet, she grasped a tube of aloe vera, squeezed the clear, gooey gel onto her eager index finger, and dabbed it onto her cheeks and shoulders. A short puff of air released from be-tween her parted lips as her body responded to the soothing salve.

Pulling at the knob on the bottom drawer of her vanity, Jennie reached for the hairdryer that had become an integral part of her morning ritual. She plugged it into the wall socket, bent at the waist and threw her head toward the floor, running her fingers through her damp hair. She would dry it at the roots and part way down the shaft, leaving the damp ends to form natural banana curls. Although she had lost a lot of hair, it was naturally thick, and the thinning would be hardly noticeable. She flipped the switch on the side of the handle and heard a pop, followed by the acrid scent of burning wire. She shrugged her shoulders, slipped into her robe and then visibly stiffened, biting her lips in defiance. "This isn't happening," she muttered as she exited the bathroom and headed toward the worn pine-plank stairs that de-scended to the lower level. Turning right, she entered the living room.

A stack of folded newspapers lay on the floor beside the Nantucket blue and ivory plaid wingback chair that Doug sat stretched-out in, feet atop the matching ottoman. He lowered the travel section long enough to plant a peck on Jennie's lips and say his morning greetings, took a sip from his half-empty coffee cup, and returned to the article that he had become engrossed in. "I'll help you with breakfast in a minute." Doug offered.

Jennie headed toward the coffee pot on the kitchen counter. Along the way she passed Aiden's battery-operated video game that he had absentmindedly laid on an end table. For some reason, it activated and started firing lasers at pop-up enemies all by itself. It had never done that before, and this gave Jennie the creeps. "I must be electrically charged today!" Jennie exclaimed as she continued on to the coffee pot, poured herself a steaming cup of French roast, returned to the living room, and took a seat on the sofa. Focusing for an instant on the blue-tinged flames licking at the pyramid of cord wood piled on the hearth, Jennie contemplated her disconcerting morning. Aiden's game had rattled her, and she needed to find a distraction to take her mind off the moment.

Moments later, Doug dropped the classifieds beside his chair and headed for the refrigerator. He peeled thick strips of maple-cured bacon from the plastic-covered slab and lined them up on the hot cast iron griddle. Jennie joined him and measured pancake mix, eggs, and milk into a stainless steel bowl as the bacon bubbled and spattered. Next, she assembled the hand-held mixer, plugged it into the receptacle, and pushed the beaters into the mixture, adjusting the speed to low. The mixer emitted a whining sound and then died with a loud pop. The acrid scent of burning wire assaulted Jennie's nostrils as a river of dread passed through her body.

"It's about time that relic went to the dump," Doug joked as Aiden appeared from the adjacent hallway. Nothing could bring Aiden out of a deep sleep like the scent of bacon wafting into his bedroom.

"Good morning, Aiden!" Jennie forced a smile, in spite of her rapidly descending mood. "How'd you sleep?"

"I feel like I've been up all night," Aiden replied. "You know how I never believed in UFOs? Well, last night changed my mind. Now I know they're real."

"What brought that up?" Jennie inquired, feeling her insides go hollow. "Were you up half the night watching some sci-fi show on T.V.?"

"No." Aiden's eyes narrowed and his face darkened. "You know what I mean," he hissed, turning on his heel and disappearing in the direction of his bedroom.

"No, I don't know what you mean," Jennie's voice trailed as she stepped away from the kitchen counter. "Aiden, what happened last night?"

Doug caught her arm. "Let him go. It's just his age," he grinned.

Ignoring Doug's advice, Jennie stomped down the hall and stood in Aiden's doorway. "What was that all about?"

"Wake up, Mom. You know what it's about."

"No, I don't. What are you talking about?" Jennie feigned ignorance.

"Just let me sleep, Mom," Aiden pleaded lifting his head from his pillow just long enough to confirm Jennie's gnawing suspicion. Blood! An abduction!

Without speaking, Jennie turned and headed up the stairs toward Sarah's bedroom, gently pushing on the half-opened door. Sarah was awake, staring at the intricate design in the antique tin ceiling. "Hi, Mom," she said as she raised a sleepy head. "I almost woke you up in the middle of the night, because a helicopter woke me up. It was right outside my bedroom window, shining a light into my eyes. When I got up and looked outside, I could see the windows and the people looking back at me. I thought that it was going to crash into the house, but then, for some reason I felt really sleepy and just fell back asleep."

"Oh," Jennie responded, "Do you think that it might just have been a dream?"

"It seemed too real to be a dream, Mom. The funny thing is, I fell asleep right away and dreamed that this funny little man took me into a little building out behind the house, and played games with me all night."

"That sounds like a fun dream, Miss Sarah," Jennie responded, spying a spot of crimson on her pillow.

"The funny thing is, Mom, I feel exhausted—like I haven't slept at all."

"Sounds like I'd better let you sleep in this morning." Jennie's voice trembled as she choked back the tears that were suddenly welling up inside of her. "I'll see you when you wake up."

Jennie closed Sarah's door and headed toward the stairs fighting back the waves of sobs that were beginning to wrack her body. By the time she reached the living room, she flung herself prostrate on the sofa and buried her face in the throw pillow, clenching her fists. Tears poured out of her as she sobbed uncontrollably. "Not my kids." Her whole body writhed in heaves of anger and despair.

"What's wrong?" She felt Doug's tender hand upon her shoulder, as he turned her toward him and held her in his arms, patting her back. Then, pushing her back far enough to look into her eyes, his perplexed voice spoke. "Why are you crying?"

"They took the kids," Jennie choked, barely audible. "There's blood on everyone's pillow."

"Who took the kids? What blood? The kids are right here in their beds. There, there…It's gonna be alright," Doug assured her.

Jennie Henderson is a real person and this is the story that she told me in the dining room of her country home more than a dozen years ago, through intermittent tears and moments of despair. She is a long-term, multigenerational experiencer, and her alien abduction events are currently ongoing.

10

Investigator
Meets Witness

By the turn of the 21st century, Jennie was committed to healing the emotional wounds caused by alien abduction and years of denial. She could no longer reject the idea that intruders had intervened in her life and wreaked havoc with her children. Intrusive memories pierced her consciousness for so many years that she didn't know quite where to begin and who to trust with her secrets.

Her 1988 abduction had left her with debilitating fatigue, weight loss, periodic memory problems, fevers, night sweats, migraine headaches, and balance problems. It came on almost immediately after the event, and had waxed and waned for years. She feared the consequences of confiding in her physicians the secret that she concealed, but she was eventually handed a chronic fatigue and immune dysfunction syndrome diagnosis.

CFIDS, a debilitating illness, is highly prevalent among alien abduction experiencers. Denise and I had become aware of this perplexing problem several years ago, when another researcher investigated it. Our recent research study, designed to identify commonalities among abduction experiencers, asked the question, "Have you been diagnosed as having chronic fatigue syndrome or reactivated mononucleosis?" Of the 50 respondents, 38 percent answered in the affirmative, whereas the figure is less than 1 percent of the general population.

The disorder is characterized by debilitating fatigue that is not improved by bed rest, and may be exacerbated by physical or mental activity. Its symptoms include profound exhaustion, problems with concentration and short-term memory, flu-like symptoms, fever, night sweats, tender lymph nodes, sore throat, and headache. Word-finding problems, reading retention difficulties, ambulation difficulty due to balance problems, lightheadedness, and mental fogginess are all symptoms of CFIDS. Medical researchers have noted immune, neurological, and endocrine abnormalities in CFIDS sufferers. Among sufferers, 25 percent are bedridden and 50 percent cannot work during flare-ups. It is not a psychiatric disorder.[1]

She'd spoken to an abduction researcher, years earlier, and to my aunt, Betty Hill. But her nagging fears had waxed and waned in concert with the anomalous events that troubled her from time to time. She wasn't attempting to convince anyone that her experiences were real, only to speak with a non-judgmental listener who might understand the implications of what she was going through and lend her a little support, knowledge, and understanding. Her proximity to my New Hampshire home made it possible for her to meet with me on a flexible basis. It also facilitated my ability to support her should any emotional needs arise during this process.

At the time, I was a field investigator for the Mutual UFO Network and the organization's Director of Field Investigator Training. As such, I specialized in alien abduction. I'd been with MUFON for several years and thought that it was a fine organization. Its dedicated members volunteer their free time to investigate UFO sightings and abductions, and collect the data for use by researchers worldwide. Their goal is to promote research on UFOs to discover the true nature of the phenomenon, with an eye toward scientific breakthroughs, improving life on our planet, and educating the public on the UFO phenomenon and its potential impact on society.[2]

Although my aunt had given Jennie guidance years earlier, it was confidential and I wasn't aware of it. Jennie knew of my research interest in UFO abductions primarily because I had been speaking about my aunt and uncle's 1961 alien abduction. I was actively researching and investigating their case and slowly writing my book with Stanton T. Friedman, *Captured! The Betty and Barney Hill UFO Experience* (Career

Press/New Page Books 2007). I had taught classes on the history of UFO abductions in the public interest section at our local high school and was recognized as a UFO abduction investigator in Rockingham County, New Hampshire. Jennie's knowledge of my aunt and uncle's abduction experience led her to contact my Aunt Betty and, years later, me. I was busy researching their case, but also allowed time to work with suspected abduction experiencers.

Healthy skepticism seems the best approach to me. I collect and evaluate whatever evidence I can acquire and withhold judgment on the reality of a witness's experiences, unless the evidence is overwhelming, and it usually is not. But I also understand that abductees are people who have lived through traumatic anomalous experiences. A sympathetic ear from a knowledgeable person is often all people need to cope with their experiences and move on productively.

Many people feel that they have no one to turn to who will believe them. The hopeless feeling that comes after an abduction experience causes despair, knowing that no one wants to hear what they have to say, that no one will take them seriously. They don't know why it happened or what it was all about. They are looking for information and a non-judgmental ear. I am one of the few people that straddle the line between advocate and investigator, offering compassion and understanding, while quietly evaluating the evidence.

After speaking with Jennie over the telephone, I agreed to speak with her in person. Her intelligence, no-nonsense approach, and conscious recall of encountering non-human entities gave me a sense that she was genuine. For many years, she'd documented her encounters in writing. This is something that I advise all experiencers to do, along with the collection of evidence and photographs. There was also physiological evidence, missing time, and witnesses. We scheduled a face-to-face interview the following week in order to record her biographical history and a detailed account of her 1988 experience. The meeting spanned nearly four hours. It would be the first of many.

When an individual reports a UFO sighting or alien abduction experience, an abduction investigator must evaluate the veracity of his or her claim. Some witnesses want to grandstand and dominate the conversation, not permitting the investigator to ask pertinent questions.

This turns investigators off, because it is nearly impossible to inter-rogate a dominant, uncooperative witness. A few witnesses have com-plained to me that they were not successful in their attempts to have their case investigated. I have found that several of the individuals in question wanted to run the show and reward the diligent investigator with the grand prize: their abduction experience. This was not Jennie.

Others are convinced that their alien visitors have given them earth-shattering messages that must immediately be conveyed to world leaders, lest the world end abruptly. I've found that the messages are usually consistent with the reporter's personal religious or politi-cal beliefs. Deadlines pass and no cataclysmic events occur. This was not Jennie.

Some suspected abductees report that they have no conscious re-call of ever observing an unconventional flying object or its crew. They have lifelong memories of terrifying monsters that come in the night. Over and over again, they wake up paralyzed, unable to move any-thing except their eyes. Shadowy figures, geometric shapes, or disem-bodied faces hover above them. They are terrified. Their hearts pound and they have difficulty breathing, as if a heavy weight is resting upon their chests. Then suddenly they find that they are able to move. There is no evidence that anything unusual has occurred. With a little educa-tion, they realize it was only sleep paralysis. This was not Jennie.

Some suspected abductees report that they have had lifelong en-counters with benevolent alien visitors. During the lonely nights in their orphanages or foster homes, they were visited by extraterrestrial beings that showed compassion toward them. No one on Earth made them feel this important. They had been abused, neglected, and aban-doned by their biological parents. They harbor tumultuous memories of stress, conflict, tension and psychosocial trauma that occurred early in their lives, and as a result, developed other realities and a dissocia-tive coping mechanism. This was not Jennie.

I do not mean to imply that all individuals who were abused as children are experiencing imaginary abductions. I know a remarkable woman who suffered horrific abuse as a child. She survived vicious beatings by using dissociation as a coping mechanism to separate the physical body from the emotional and physical pain that was being inflicted upon her. This coping mechanism carried the child to an astral realm, and when the child returned to the physical body a special gift was delivered—psychic mediumship. Today this individual carries her gift to police departments to solve crimes against children. This is not imaginary. Forensic drawings are sketched and crimes are solved as a direct result of psychic intervention.

Many suspected abductees shudder and their voices tremble when they speak of their suspected abduction experience. They choke back tears between hesitant words. Their previously normal lives have been disrupted. They had never been given to fantasy. They aren't seeking attention. They've stared terror in the face and have emerged feeling confused, perplexed, and emotionally traumatized. They still cannot believe that it has happened to them. They question their own memories and wonder if there is a prosaic explanation. They are seeking help from someone who knows more than they do about alien abduction. This was Jennie.

She cautioned me that she didn't want to engage in a formal investigation. It was too risky. She and her husband were prominent members of her community and had too much to lose should their information, somehow, become public. (For this reason, I have fictionalized any information that might reveal their identities.) She knew about the violation of confidentiality that had thrust Betty and Barney Hill into the limelight, and wanted no part of it.

Initially, I was somewhat amused by Jennie's biographical history. She is a Baby Boomer, who admits that she simply didn't fit the stereotypical image of her peers. She didn't dream the good life on a communal farm. Having grown up on a small farm, she was no stranger to the physical labor that comes with agricultural work. You might think of her as a throwback to an earlier more conservative generation, except for the very strange tale she has to tell of alien abduction.

Jennie is now the happily married mother of two grown children from a long line of New England poultry farmers. Their roots in the northeast date back to the 17th century British migration. Family lore has it that her British great-grandfather married a woman from the Penobscot nation. Her great-grandfather fled with his parents to

America during the Irish potato famine. Sparkling green eyes and wavy copper hair suggest that she favors the Celtic side of her family.

She is the third of five children born to a stable, stay-at-home mother and a father who split his time between the family farm and a small trade-oriented business. It was a happy household, with many visitors stopping in throughout the day for coffee and conversation. Jennie was well-loved and had a strong sense of community connectedness, partly because of her family's involvement in the community church. But despite her youthful security, unsettling memories of alien intrusion had created a feeling of "weirdness" for Jennie late in her teens.

Her school records indicate that she was an above-average student and popular among her classmates. More of a social butterfly than a scholar, Jennie admits that she could have achieved more if she had applied herself. Yet despite her perceived deficits, her report cards indicate that she was a conscientious student. She says that her ability to absorb and retain information changed at age 14, when she awoke one morning feeling like a new, fully aware person. It was as if someone had suddenly activated synapses in her brain that had long been dormant. She developed a nearly photographic memory and experienced an academic awakening. Throughout her secondary school years, she excelled, retaining detailed memories of facts and figures. Her memory was remarkable, and this reflected in her grades. Jennie suspected that it was during this timeframe that her frightening nocturnal intrusions began.

After high school, she attended a small liberal arts college and graduated with a degree in secondary education. Following graduation, she found a teaching position in a small mountain community in upstate New Hampshire. This afforded her the opportunity to participate in the winter sports that she loved and to spend the summer hiking along the granite-dotted slopes.

She met her first husband, Tom, a young real estate developer, not long after she arrived in town. She caught his eye that winter as she struggled on a black diamond trail, having overestimated her skiing ability. He had rescued her by offering instruction that improved her technique and facilitated her journey to the base lodge. They married two years later and had a son and daughter. Tragically, her husband lost his life in an automobile accident when the children were 2 and 4.

Jennie took her children back to her hometown in the southern part of the state, and the support of family and lifelong friends. It was there that she reunited with a childhood sweetheart, now a successful small business owner. They married 30 months later.

She and her second husband, Doug, had achieved a comfortable lifestyle and settled down to a contented and secure middle-class existence. He was actively involved in small town politics and served on several committees. Her children were good students and active in the community. She had seemingly boundless energy. In addition to her work as an educator, Jennie was the heart of the home. She gave it the pulse that kept all of its many activities organized and flowing. It was a happy home. But the events that she experienced one winter night in early 1988 brought down everything in her secure world. Her life would never be quite the same.

Jennie had sought a prosaic explanation for her strange experiences. She is a natural skeptic. The best explanation that she could find was hypnagogic/hypnopompic hallucinations: vivid visual, auditory, or tactile events that occur at the transition between wakefulness and sleep or sleep and waking up.[3] She wondered if she had simply confused internally generated imagery for real events. Sure, the trauma seemed real, but she hoped it was fantasy-based, triggered by the rapid firing of neural synapses in concert with visual and auditory hallucinations. Similar imagery had been created in experimental sleep labs, but it lacked the details of Jennie's experience, the additional witnesses, and the physiological evidence.

Jennie's suspected abduction memories and the anxiety she was experiencing had driven her to contact Dr. James Harder, a prominent UFO and abduction researcher, specializing in close encounter cases and UFO propulsion systems. He had earned his PhD in fluid mechanics and was a professor of engineering, with responsibilities in bioengineering, at the University of California, Berkeley. His primary interests were in applied mathematics and digital simulation, sediment transport mechanics, feedback control systems, and artificial internal organs. He was also a certified hypnotist with experience assisting suspected abductees. He was one of six scientists asked to testify on UFOs before the U.S. House of Representatives Committee on Science and Astronautics in 1968.

I had spoken with him several times during his visits to my aunt Betty Hill's home. Through the years, he visited Betty and my family from time to time. They became close friends during the 1970s, when he was working on a project to determine the prevalence of alien abduction among biological relatives. He interviewed several members of my own family, and he hypnotized a few to learn more about their UFO encounters, including a landing on my grandparent's farm. I admired him and learned from him through personal contact and occasional correspondence.

Jennie met Jim during one of his visits to New Hampshire. She had begun to experience anxiety and sleeplessness after the residents of her apartment building observed a UFO hovering low near her bedroom window. She wasn't there when it occurred, but was startled, upon returning home, to find her neighbors gathered excitedly outside their apartment building. They had been attempting to find her, but hadn't realized that she was still working at a part-time second job.

The following morning her visibly shaken roommate was nervously scurrying around the apartment opening and closing closet doors. She walked into Jennie's room and asked, "What in hell happened here last night?" When Jennie feigned ignorance, she replied, "I don't know what it was, but it was *weird*!" Vague memories of contact with non-human entities flooded Jennie's consciousness. She rose from bed to find that her apartment door stood wide open and her dog was outside tearing up the neighborhood. Her roommate denied opening it. Two weeks later and without warning, the roommate packed up and moved to California, stating that she could no longer remain in such a weird environment. She felt compelled to get out of there—and fast.

Jennie had nowhere to run to. She had commitments, a new boyfriend, and a stable job. Intrusive memories flooded her thoughts. Although she had been sleeping well prior to that fateful night, she suddenly developed insomnia, panic attacks, and a fear of being alone at night. For these reasons, she sought assistance from Dr. Harder.

Dr. Harder interviewed Jennie about her memories of the night in question. He then performed a hypnotic induction, sharpening her focus and strengthening her recall. When he instructed her to return to the source of her anxiety regarding the night in question, she recalled standing on her balcony, accompanied by a being that she was not able to describe. Swiftly, she and her escort were floated aboard a craft to a small, dimly lit room with at least one rounded wall. She was directed to position herself in a semi-reclining apparatus that reminded her of a spindly dentist's chair without the padding and sturdy framework. A tall, thin, non-human entity with large, faceted, insect-like eyes entered the room. The being positioned his face within inches of hers and stared into her eyes. At that instant, she felt the most intense sensation of pure love that she had ever known. But what happened next was troubling, and she didn't want to recall it. Dr. Harder skillfully led her away from the experience.

A relieved Jennie thanked Dr. Harder for his assistance, because she was now certain that her troubling memories were only a dream, stating that levitation is impossible, so her experience couldn't have been real. It violated the laws of physics. His response burned in her mind like a red hot poker. It was indeed possible, even probable, as far as he was concerned. The majority of abductees were making similar reports. Jennie was stunned, but she didn't voice her swelling anxiety to Dr. Harder. He suggested, with her approval, that she would be able to recall the details of subsequent abductions if and only if the emotional impact wasn't too troubling. Unfortunately, any memory of alien intrusion was troubling to Jennie. The memories that came forth over and over again were startling and disquieting. Never before had she experienced so much fear and anxiety. What had previously seemed like a small event mushroomed into a toxic cloud that enveloped her thoughts and feelings.

She had sought comfort and understanding, but was left with apprehension until her nocturnal visitations ceased. Eventually, her anxiety diminished and she was able to lead a normal life, without the fear of falling asleep at night. But the January 16, 1988 intrusive event left her feeling perplexed, helpless, and physically ill.

· · · · · · · · · · · · · ·

11

Taking the Bull
by the Horns

Nearly 25 years after Jennie's hypnosis session with Dr. James Harder, she made the decision to square off with the intrusive memories that had troubled her for so long. She confessed to me that try as she might, she couldn't cast off her perplexing memories of the night of January 16, 1988. It left her feeling violated, angry, and bewildered. She complained that her recollections, whether real or dreamed, were distressing. The very idea of being abducted repeatedly made her blood run cold. Her inability to bring these experiences to an end or to temper the fear that was increasingly affecting her mood left her feeling helpless.

Unresolved emotional trauma is common among abduction experiencers. When a person is forced to suppress memories that aren't socially acceptable, they tend to increase in magnitude. Often, mental health counselors are not aware of the constellation of symptoms affecting abduction experiencers, such as fear of falling asleep, the inability to remain asleep, the feeling of having been violated, the anger that comes when one is taken against one's will, the heightened sense of awareness,[1] the gynecological problems among women (infections, missing fetuses, perforated vaginal walls, etc.), the increased sensitivity to light, the prevalence of chronic fatigue and immune dysfunction syndrome (a debilitating illness that affects nearly 40 percent of abduction experiencers), the malfunctions of electrical equipment, and the scoop marks, burns, florescence, and strange bruises left on abduction experiencer's bodies.[2]

Based upon my conversations with abduction experiencers, I have found that study groups that guarantee anonymity do more to help abduction experiencers than psychological counseling, especially for those who desire support from like-minded people. Numerous academic studies have demonstrated that those who meet the criteria for having experienced a real abduction (e.g. witnesses, evidence, conscious recall) are no more likely to be suffering from psychological disturbance than the general population. This group of individuals benefits most when they can speak about their events to non-judgmental listeners who share the same type of experience. Knowledge, understanding, and acceptance lead to healing.

People in Jennie's position have voiced to me that they have no interest in proving to scientists that their abductions are real. They only want support and understanding from like-minded people who will protect their identity and allow communication in a safe environment. Hypnosis facilitates memory, which is important to most people, even though the risk of confabulating false memories is possible. The Marden-Stoner study revealed that most abduction experiencers have conscious, continuous recall of at least part of their experience. For this reason, they believe that it was real.

After studying the academic research, I had been extremely reticent about the use of hypnosis to recover repressed memories. There has been abundant skepticism about the ability of trance subjects to differentiate between real and imagined information recovered through hypnosis. Cognitive science studies have demonstrated that hypnosis is not a surefire method of recovering accurate memories. It is the malleability of memory and the fallibility of hypnosis that has cast it in a poor light. Under hypnosis, the truth is what the participant subjectively perceives. This may or may not be consistent with the objective non-personal truth. Although the general experience might have been recalled accurately, when no detailed information exists, confabulated material might fill in the blanks. This is especially true when an inexperienced hypnotist asks leading questions. For this reason, we cannot assume that hypnotically recovered memories reflect real events unless there is confirmation in the form of evidence and/or independent witnesses.

Hypnosis was used effectively to retrieve detailed memories of abduction experiences in the Betty and Barney Hill UFO abduction case. Dr. Benjamin Simon, a prominent psychiatrist who specialized in deep trance hypnosis saw the Hills separately each weekend for several months. At the end of each session, he reinstated amnesia. This was done for two reasons: first, to reduce the emotional impact of their recovered memories of a traumatic abduction by non-humans, and second, to prevent them from discussing their hypnotically retrieved memories and contaminating each other's information. The Hills emerged from the experience with reasonably consistent details of a shared experience, if one allows for variations in their speech patterns and personalities. However, some dream-generated memories, such as a discussion about Betty's favorite foods and the color yellow that seemed not to be in the ET's vocabulary, might possibly been added to Betty's hypnotic recall as confabulated, fantasy-generated information.

Investigators and hypnotherapists working with abduction experiencers must strive to avoid causing them additional mental or physical harm. This is difficult, because the nature of abduction itself is usually traumatic. Therefore, we must caution ourselves that the recall of traumatic memories might bring about changes in attitude and behavior that could be either harmful or beneficial.[3] Considering the fact that false memories might be created by the hypnotic subject's exposure to abduction media, biographical accounts of other's experiences, or dreams, we must proceed cautiously.

It is natural for experiencers to be curious about their encounters. Jennie's curiosity led her to read several books, including *The Interrupted Journey*, John G. Fuller's 1966 book about Betty and Barney Hill's UFO encounter and subsequent alien abduction; *Fire in the Sky* (1996) by Travis Walton, *Communion* (1987) by Whitley Strieber, and *Missing Time* (1987) by the late abduction researcher Budd Hopkins. Her reading had exposed Jennie to the risk of confabulating, but it was something that we had to acknowledge and attempt to moderate. She had also attended a few lectures by UFO researchers and a symposium. However, she had kept a journal of her abduction memories, and it predated anything she'd read on the subject except the Hill's UFO abduction. I had to weigh the possibility that Jennie might create a false experience under hypnosis against the fact that she had experienced missing time in her younger years, had witnesses who observed a UFO in close proximity to her home, and physiological evidence, plus medical records that bore out her story. I cautioned her not to read additional information about UFO abductions or to investigate it on the Internet.

An assessment of risk is an essential prerequisite to determine that an underlying psychiatric illness or personality/behavioral disorder is not present.[4] Rushing into hypnosis with the assumption that it is the best method of resolving abduction-related trauma is, in my opinion, very risky business. It could exacerbate an underlying disorder and cause the deterioration of the mental well-being of an individual who, until that point, was maintaining his or her mental illness.

I inquired about Jennie's emotional history, looking for red flags that might indicate emotional instability or a psychiatric disorder. Aside from her abduction memories, her life had been stable and productive. She and her children had entered into grief counseling after the untimely death of her first husband, and she had made an excellent adjustment to her new life as a widow with young children. When she moved back to her childhood home, she gained the support of her parents, but did not become overly dependent upon them. She found employment and became self-sufficient. After an adequate recovery period, she met and eventually married Doug. Their marriage was stable and mutually gratifying.

I had come to know Jennie as a down-to-earth, well-balanced, realistic woman. But before I agreed to do her hypnosis sessions, I asked her to complete a battery of psychological screening devices. The screening measures were designed to identify a tendency toward fantasy proneness, altered realities, temporal lobe lability, dissociation, a negative or abusive early childhood history, emotional functioning, mood fluctuations, and so on. Her scores placed her squarely within the normal range of functioning on every measure. She showed no sign of psychological instability or personality disorder.

The next step was to consider whether hypnosis would be in Jennie's best interest. As I stated earlier, I am very apprehensive about opening up memories that might prove to be traumatic. But Jennie was determined to gain greater insight into the abduction memories that were part of her conscious, continuous recall.

My decision to work with Jennie was a difficult one to make. I explained to her that although many people assume that memories retrieved through hypnosis are substantially accurate, it is generally understood by professionals that it is impossible to determine the historical accuracy of memories obtained through regressive hypnosis, regardless of the intensity of emotional expression. I also informed Jennie that the mainstream scientific literature has established that hypnotically retrieved memories are often not reliable. Despite this forewarning, Jennie signed an informed consent agreement and underwent hypnotic suggestibility testing. Years after our first meeting, her first session commenced.

Before her first hypnotic regression, we spent time conditioning her to enter into a deep hypnotic trance. Jennie had to learn to let go of her apprehension and to relax and accept my suggestions. Deepening techniques were employed, and she was given a safe haven to retreat to if her memories became uncomfortably frightening.

There is an interesting characteristic of hypnosis that most laymen are not aware of: not everyone can be hypnotized. Those who lack the ability to focus and attend will not be compliant enough to enter into a hypnotic state. A person who is overly nervous or who doesn't trust the hypnotist will be resistant to hypnosis. Even after the hypnotic subject enters into a hypnotic trance, he or she will not be under the hypnotist's control. All hypnosis is, in a sense, is self-hypnosis. It is not a mystical process, but instead is only an altered state of consciousness—not sleeping or being unconscious.

Hypnosis makes it possible for the hypnotist to speak to the person's subconscious mind to offer suggestions or to recall forgotten information. But the person must be motivated to comply. No one can make a hypnotized person do anything against his or her will. Although hypnosis isn't dangerous, the misuse of hypnosis by unqualified persons, especially when traumatic memories are recalled, can be. In my opinion, it is extremely important for the hypnotist and the hypnotic subject to be present in the same room. The hypnotist must be alert to the client's body language and emotional state at all times and prepared to intervene with calming suggestions.

After several hours of working together, I facilitated Jennie's hypnotic regression to the day before her January 1988 experience. She spoke of her day as a mother, teacher, and wife. She was looking forward to spending a well-deserved, extended weekend at home with her family. They had spent Friday evening together watching a movie, while eating popcorn in their family room. They turned in at 11 and had a restful night's sleep.

I guided Jennie through Saturday's activities up to the night that had left her with such troubling memories. In an account rich with descriptive detail, Jennie recalled spending the evening at home, surrounded by her children, husband, and dog. A crackling fire warmed the family room as the children reclined in blanket rolls on the carpeted floor. They had relaxed in front of the TV set watching *The Karate Kid*. Jennie moved forward to the time that she and Doug decided to call it a night. They had turned in earlier than usual, anticipating a restful sleep after sending their children off to their own bedrooms.

Moving on, Jennie suddenly shrieks, "Oh...I got woken up by my dog. She's barking and barking and barking." A little calmer now, she says, "Oh God, why is she barking? She's going to wake everyone up. And then all of a sudden, she stops. She doesn't wind down. She doesn't do anything. She just stops. I think that she woke Sarah up because there is someone in my room. Is Sarah scared? Is she sick? I don't know. So, I'm waiting. She's probably going to come around to my side of the bed. And Doug.... No something is wrong. It's not Sarah. Doug gets up, and he's put back down in bed. And he's not moving. And I'm up and I'm looking."

Jennie's tone of voice and body language signal me that this was a frightening memory, so I offer calming suggestions to her and remind her that she could go back to a safe place at any time, or proceed with her story. I told her that if she continued, she'd be all right to tell me about her experience. Nothing could harm her now. She wants to proceed with her story.

Jennie's body language tells me that she is on alert. There is somebody in the room and she sees its eyes. She moans and continues, "I

Jennie's sketch of being transported to the waiting UFO.

thought that this was over. But they're back. And they're down by the foot of my bed. There are three of them. I can see their eyes. They are shining...glistening. They have glistening eyes. I don't want this to go on again. And.... Don't!" She screams. Using my most soothing voice, I reassure Jennie that nothing can harm her now, that she can relax and take a deep breath. Her body relaxes and she calms down. I then ask her to proceed if she wants to.

Jennie sobs, "Don't! Don't! Don't!" I calm her again, reassuring her that she is safe and can get through it. She will be all right. She becomes aware that paralysis has swept over her body. She wants to escape, but finds that she can't move. I offer calming suggestions again. "Relax. Take a deep breath. You can get through this. It is going to be all right."

Jennie takes a deep breath and gasps in distress, "I'm up! I'm moving! I'm up. I was lying down but all of sudden, I'm up." She instantaneously shifts from a reclining position to an upright position under someone else's control. At that moment, Jennie's body arches and only her head and heels remain on the couch in my office. She continues, "I'm going toward the window through to the outside. There is a huge window in my bedroom. I'm going right through that window. They are around me." There is one being above her and she is accompanied by two others.

A moment later, she finds herself inside a lighted hallway with a non-human escort who seems uncannily familiar to her. Her mood shifts from intense fear to calmness. She is now in a familiar environment with the escort she has seen throughout her lifetime. He stands across the narrow curved hallway, and not wanting to look at him, she lowers her head.

Next, she realizes that her children have appeared and are escorted down a dimly lit hallway by gray beings with large fluid eyes. Jennie observes a small division between the hallways. It is one continuous hallway, but there is a division between the front section and the back hallway that leads to the examining rooms. The rear hallway seems darker.

She is ushered to a small, dimly lit room with at least one rounded wall and ceiling, where she is instructed to lie down on a small rectangular table. There are at least three additional entities in the room.

Their physical appearance is a little different than that of her escort. Their heads and eyes are a little larger in proportion to the size of their bodies and they are shorter. They line up against a wall and seem to fade into the darkness, not participating in the procedures that she is being subjected to. She senses that their primary function is to act as guards and assistants.

She also detects a male entity at the foot of the table, but she isn't able to get a good look at him. She begins to describe the procedure she was forced to endure. "I'm lying on the table and they're going to do something that I don't want them to do...." She exclaims and winces in pain after feeling a bodily sensation. I calm her again and give her permission to retreat from her memories or to move on. She decides to continue. "They communicate to me that I am performing an important function for them. It is helping them to understand more about us. And they need to take my genetic material." She cries out as if in pain, and I advise her that she won't feel it now. She can feel calm and quietly observe what she perceives is occurring. Time has passed and the examiner produces another instrument. Jennie states, "They have this...it's like a probe, and there is a wire or a tube connected to it. I think it is something about vibrational frequency. They have to stimulate my harmonic...vibrational frequency. I don't know what they're talking about."

I am perplexed, so I and ask her to explain why she thinks that they are attempting to alter her vibrational frequency. Jennie replies, "I can hear it in my head. They have this probe...." She cries out. "There is a pulse that moves up through my body—almost like a vibration. It's a little painful. I feel a tingling energy passing though me. There is energy moving though me." Jennie senses a tingling vibration pulsing through her body over and over again. "They are happy.... No, I can't say that they're happy. They are pleased with the progress that they are seeing."

Jennie's escort stands by her head during the entire procedure. When she cries out in pain, he touches her temples and her pain subsides. Her escort remains in the room with her when the procedure is finished, but the doctor and possibly the guards exit.

Jennie continues, "I think that I'm alone with my escort now, but I'm looking only at him and the wall with the lights. The guards are lined up against a different wall, but I don't look in that direction." The lights appear to be tiny buttons beneath a rectangular obsidian panel on the wall. Jennie is seated on the table and her escort is standing to her right, facing her.

When I inquire about Jennie's mood, she states, "I am pleased and he is pleased...if it's a he, or whatever it is. It's over now and I can just wait and I can relax. I have served my purpose.... I have a lesson to learn. That lesson is that the completely human Jennie is very frightened by them, but there is no need to be, because he shows me how kind they are to me. He makes an image appear so I can see how kind they are to me. There is no reason to fear. I need to learn that they are doing no harm. I am part of them. Before I was born they inserted a tiny fragment of themselves into me. "

This reassurance by her abductors is consistent with the alien abduction process. It is common for abduction experiencers to feel that they have been manipulated into feeling loved by their captors. Many feel that it is a deceptive act to control the abductee's behavior by beings that are serving their own purpose and have no compassion for their human experimental subjects. But others feel a strong bond with what they perceive to be benevolent visitors from another planet. I have often wondered why the escort waits until the abductee is experiencing pain to offer desensitization. Why not give the patient anesthesia before the painful procedure begins?

Jennie received a visual image of a dying planet that had long ago been teeming with life. She perceives that it was her escort's home that had been all but destroyed hundreds—if not thousands—of years ago by a predatory invader. His people had attempted to defend themselves, but in doing so, the surface of their planet was destroyed. The survivors were forced to move below the surface into an underground network of connected tunnels and buildings. She looked upon it with great sadness.

When Jennie's procedure and lesson are finished, she is returned to the hallway by her escort. He stands near the inside wall of the corridor while Jennie stands closer to the outside wall. Her eyes are focused downward, as if studying the floor in order to avoid looking at him. She is amazed to find a discolored streak. She thought that such advanced beings would have been able to produce a flawless craft.

She waits for a few seconds until her two youngsters emerge from around the corner. Her next memory is of waking up in bed. She feels wiped out—completely drained. There is blood on her pillow and her eyes are inflamed and stinging. She finds painful triangle-shaped wounds on her upper back and still carries the scars. She can offer no prosaic explanation for her symptoms and suspects that it is the direct result of the procedure they subjected her to aboard the craft.

An explanation for Jennie's experience cannot be found in the tenets of Western scientific thought. Our current scientific paradigms dictate that we must apply Occam's razor to Jennie's experience. Occam's razor dictates that the simplest explanation is probably correct. Using Occam's razor, and if we ignore the testimony of Jennie and her children, taken with the physiological evidence, we would be forced to conclude that Jennie had an imaginary experience or a dream that she recalled or embellished during her hypnosis session. However, it is scientifically dishonest, in my opinion, to ignore the evidence and pretend it doesn't exist. There were witnesses and physiological evidence that cannot be denied. My experience has led me to the conclusion that some abduction phenomena cannot be fully understood within the tenets of Western scientific thought. Too many credible witnesses have reported specific details of little known phenomena to me. I can no longer ignore their testimony and the evidence they offer in support of it.

The vast majority of credible abduction experiencers describe one of two physical sensations during their transport on and off the craft. They feel a rhythmic, pulsing energy that might begin as being somewhat painful, or as if every cell in their body is coming apart. This physical sensation gives us insight into Jennie's statement that she felt a tingling, pulsing energy coursing through her body, as well the ET's communication that they were attempting to increase her harmonic vibrational frequency. This, taken with the fact that it is commonplace for abduction experiencers to report that they have been transported through a solid object, such as a window, wall, or roof, just as Jennie reported, led me to a theory that can only be found in theoretical physics.

I am not a physicist, so I decided to consult with one. To my amazement I learned that all of this is theoretically possible.

In theory, all matter resonates at a vibrational frequency. Solid inanimate objects, such as rocks, vibrate at a lower frequency than animate objects, such as animals. If the object vibrates at a high enough frequency its energized particles will become energetically invisible or dematerialize. In order to pass a human body though a solid object both the body and the solid surface need to vibrate at an equally high frequency. The trick is to match up both frequency and phase of the human and the solid object. We have already done something like this in the laboratory. Remember, 99.9 percent of an atom is empty space between the protons and electrons, so it is just a matter of getting things in alignment to get them to inter-penetrate, making it possible for matter to pass thorough matter. Our science is only at the beginning stage of understanding this process. But imagine what a civilization 1,000 years more advanced than our own has developed. If they can travel though the vast expanse of space and survive, despite the seemingly impossible challenges on their trip to Earth, one can only wonder what other scientific discoveries have been made. In our own history of science, what once seemed like magic is today's reality.

As with any claim of alien abduction, Jennie's case must be evaluated in an unbiased manner. I was impressed with the fact that she was eager to find a viable alternative explanation for her perplexing abduction memories. Several years of reflection had allowed her to consider several prosaic causes, including dreams, hypnopompic hallucinations, and sleep paralysis.

Her children had partial recall of the events. But her husband hadn't recalled anything unusual occurring that night. This is not unusual. UFO abduction literature is bursting with accounts in which one spouse is surreptitiously taken from the conjugal bed, while the other is "switched off" in a coma-like state. Sometimes, as in Jennie's case, the nonparticipating bed partner responds by rising from bed in an attempt to fight off the nocturnal intruders. He or she is quickly paralyzed and rendered unconscious. It is possible, given the fact that this is widely reported among abductees and their families, that Doug endured the same treatment. Aside from Doug's failure to recall the experience, his two children retained conscious memories that something "weird" happened during the night.

It was Jennie's conscious recall of the events that finally caused her to reject the idea that sleep paralysis or hallucinations accounted for her memories. Her dog's canine alarm had startled her into wakefulness. She then observed figures rushing into her bedroom, and observed her husband rising in a defensive stance. Without a scuffle, he was immediately laid motionless on the bed by the figures in her bedroom. She cried out because she realized that this was the onset of an abduction, then sensed a numbing wave of paralysis sweeping up her body.

We must also take into account the physiological evidence. Some of her symptoms, such as weight loss, vomiting, sleeplessness, and hair loss could possibly be attributed to stress, but stress doesn't adequately explain her burns. Her medical reports indicate that she sought treatment for her declining health condition. Within a month of the event, her health declined to the point of being incapacitated. Unable to walk normally or to drive a car, she was forced to take a leave of absence from the job she loved and had been doing successfully for several years.

Electromagnetic anomalies are rife in UFO abduction literature. It is important to note that Jennie had never before experienced a string of power surges that caused lights and appliances to blow out when she touched them, even though she had experienced missing time and abduction recall in the past. It was a onetime event and it never occurred again. It is significant that she was the only member of her household who triggered the apparent power surges, although her husband was engaging in similar activities. Although she suspects (and recalls under hypnosis), that her children were also taken, they had no such affect.

Also, we must consider Jennie's children's behavior. They both recalled that something unusual had occurred in their home that night and that their mother was distressed. It didn't take long for Jennie to find kitchen knives and hatchets under their mattresses. It was out of character for two well-behaved, studious youngsters. They resided in a stable home with loving and supportive parents in a sleepy, secure community. This sudden shift in their behavior is perplexing but consistent with behavioral changes reported by others who have experienced alien abduction.

I cannot speak to the veridicality of Jennie's hypnotic recall aboard the craft. Hypnosis is an altered state of consciousness that narrows one's focus upon a specific event or topic. The hypnotized person can often recall long-forgotten information in great detail, but when pressured for information, false (i.e. fabricated) memories, can emerge where no real memories exist. Hypnosis facilitates a subjective memory that may or may not be consistent with objective reality. For this reason it must be used cautiously. All that can be said is that Jennie's statements about her experience on the craft explain her injuries.

・ ・ ・ ・ ・ ・ ・ ・ ・ ・ ・ ・ ・ ・

12

Early Memories

Jennie's childhood memories are filled with sun-drenched summer days spent in her family's vegetable gardens, tending to the plants that would sustain them through the entire year, or languishing on a blanket on the warm sand at the edge of the Atlantic Ocean. Hers was a large, close-knit family of parents, grandparents, aunts, uncles, and cousins who enjoyed each other's company and spent most of their time together. The winter brought sliding adventures on the hilly backlands of her grandparent's farm with her four siblings and hot chocolate loaded with marshmallows in front of a crackling fire. It was idyllic except for sporadic nocturnal intrusions that disrupted her sleep and brought terror into her otherwise peaceful nights. Her parents attributed it to early childhood nightmares brought on by the insecurity she felt having her own bedroom. But Jennie wonders if its source might have been more complex.

Her first memory of alien contact emerged during a hypnosis session with Dr. James Harder during the 1970s. He regressed her to the summer of her third year, when she recalled the warm sun beating down upon her face as she watched her mother and grandmother pick blackberries on the backlands of the family farm. She was standing judiciously next to her young brother's carriage, with her older sister watching over the youngsters a few feet from the thorny bramble. In the distance she could see a row of figures like grotesque toy soldiers lined up for inspection. She assumed that they must have been dressed in Halloween masks. In preparation for October's ghoulish event, her mother had been working with Jennie on reducing her fear of scary faces, such as clowns and witches. She cannot recall observing her mother and grandmother emerging from the blackberry patch. Her next memory is of holding her mother's hand as they came face to face with this strange group of gray-skinned creatures with oversized fluid eyes standing in a straight row, almost like a reception line. She felt proud of her big girl status, because she had not cried as she looked upon their visage.

Jennie doesn't completely trust the veracity of her early childhood memory (nor do I), but spoke of it as an improbable event. She wonders if she might have created a fantasy under hypnosis when she was asked to recall her first abduction memory. The suggestion was clearly there. She needed only to recall a real event and overlay it with a confabulated abduction memory.

The Marden-Stoner study yielded some surprising results about abduction experiences dating back to early childhood. Of the 50 experiencers, 36 percent stated that their first abduction experience occurred before age 5. Another 20 percent believe that it occurred before age 10. Only 14 percent stated that they were taken for the first time as adults and another 16 percent are not certain at what age their first abduction experience occurred. One abduction researcher recently declared that all abductees are taken at a very young age. My research suggests that those whose parents are experiencers are likely to report early childhood home abductions or visitations. But others, whose parents are not experiencers, might have been taken from an external environment at an early age while playing outside with friends, or later in life while hunting, fishing, or driving.

Memories of viewing non-human entities emerging from bedroom walls or being snatched from one's crib are ubiquitous in modern abduction literature. Skeptics wonder if it is a figment of one's primeval imagination, rooted in the collective unconscious, or a false memory confabulated while under hypnosis. But abduction experiencers say that the encounter is as real as real.

Jennie's next memory (without hypnosis), of encountering frightening non-humans occurred at age 13. She awoke one summer morning with a haunting memory from the night before. She thought that it had been a dream, but she will never forget the pain from her physical injuries. Her burning genitals wept clear fluid and her sacroiliac was too painful to tolerate sitting on a hard chair at the breakfast table. Oddly, her mother didn't question Jennie's pain, but only instructed her to place a pillow on her chair.

Upon rising, Jennie recalled a dreamlike experience of waking up on a table in what she thought was an operating room, although she had never been in one. She was surrounded by what seemed like a surgical team, but she couldn't remember any details. As Jennie's eyelids parted, she recalled her mother standing in the doorway. Frantically she sounded an alarm to the surgical team, "She's waking up! Don't let her open her eyes!" It was too late.

Nearly 30 years later, seeking a resolution to the traumatic stress that stemmed from her abduction memories and her CFIDS, Jennie relived this experience in a psychotherapist's office in a powerful abreaction, without hypnosis. Years after that, her mother tearfully confirmed what Jennie had suspected all along. She had observed Jennie's procedure during a family abduction. The event had been as traumatic for her as it had been for Jennie, but she felt that she shouldn't talk about it. At that moment, both women realized that they had been victimized by non-human entities whose behavior suggested little regard for their emotional responses or individual rights.

The damage to 13-year-old Jennie's genital-rectal area might lead to the suspicion that she had been sexually abused, possibly by someone in her own home. As an investigator, I had to inquire about this, as difficult as it was to broach the subject. Her reply was, "Not a chance." She insisted that the men in her family were respectful, mature, and morally above board. There was no substance abuse of any kind that might have caused anyone to lose their inhibitions. Her father and brothers consistently behaved appropriately toward her.

She made it perfectly clear that this was not the only time in her life that she suffered similar injuries. Periodically throughout her adult life, she awoke with vague memories of contact with non-human entities and painful bruises in her genital-rectal area. It was sometimes accompanied by blood unrelated to menses. On one occasion, she had visited her family physician to ascertain that she hadn't developed an abnormal medical condition. Her medical records indicate that her physician was concerned about her profuse clear and pink tinged discharge and performed a PAP test. The laboratory report indicates that there were no abnormalities.

Denise and I inquired about the prevalence of gynecological problems among experiencers on the "Marden-Stoner Commonalities Among Abduction Experiencers" project; 69 percent of the female respondents reported that they had experienced gynecological problems, as opposed to 33 percent of the control group. These problems included a spectrum of disorders, such as vaginal infections, vaginal puncture wounds, venereal disease in an abstinent woman, missing fetus syndrome, and hysterectomy, attributed to an abduction experience.

After her frightening dream, Jennie's bedroom presented a new problem at bedtime. Each night, she gingerly crept on tiptoes toward the double doors of her closet. With trepidation, she grasped the round brass knob on each door and in one swift movement flung them open. Satisfied that no one lurked inside her closet, she closed the doors and dashed for her light switch. As soon as she gathered enough fortitude to flip it to an off position, she raced toward her bed, diving under the covers and pulling them up over her head.

Dozens of suspected abductees have independently reported to me that they developed a sudden fear of their bedroom closet immediately following a strange experience during the night. Some reported that they observed non-human entities coming from their closet. Others developed an inexplicable fear of inanimate objects in their closet, such as bongos or drums.

Sporadically throughout her teenage years, Jennie awoke to find herself tucked tightly into bed with her feet on her pillow and her head at the foot of her bed. One night, her brother's shrieks woke Jennie and alerted the entire family that something very frightening was occurring in their home. Jennie was seated upright on her bed speaking with someone, as if carrying on a conversation, with someone in her closet. But upon inspection no one was found. It was a weird event that the family couldn't forget. A prosaic explanation might be that Jennie was simply talking in her sleep. But this was not her only unusual teenage experience.

At age 16, Jennie was a popular high school junior and class officer. She earned good grades in her college prep classes and participated in field hockey and softball. On Sundays, she supervised a group of pre-schoolers at her church while their parents attended the service. Late in the fall, at the start of the basketball season, she and a friend were on a narrow secondary road on the outskirts of town traveling to a game, when a brightly lit, teardrop-shaped object rapidly descended upon them. The young couple initially thought that a helicopter was having some fun with them, but they could not hear the roar of chopper blades.

The teens had discussed UFOs in the past, and Jennie's friend flat-out rejected the notion, despite the flap that had Southern New Hampshirites waiting under power lines night after night hoping to spot one.[1] At first glance, Jennie hadn't believed that the quickly approaching bright light was a UFO. She said she was only having some fun by provoking an emotional response in her disbelieving friend. Jennie rolled down her window and looked up as she jokingly told her friend that it was a UFO.

But what came next changed her mind. It hovered at telephone pole height above their car, and almost immediately, the car engine died. Her friend frantically attempted to restart it, and finally it did start up.

Not noticing a time lapse, the friends continued along their way to the game. The craft was nowhere in sight. For a reason that she still finds perplexing, Jennie was frantically searching for her purse. The teenagers were shocked when, upon arriving at the high school, they found that the doors were locked and the lights were turned off. Jennie had been instructed by her mother to transport her younger brother home from the game. She had planned on meeting him there.

The clock in their vehicle indicated that it was still early in the evening. (It had malfunctioned.) Neither of the friends was wearing a watch, so they stopped at a local variety store to check the time. It read nearly 11 p.m. They knew they would be in trouble with their parents. Even worse, the only explanation that Jennie could offer for her late arrival was a UFO encounter. They had no prosaic explanation for their lost time.

As she approached the front door of her farmhouse, Jennie was both perplexed and somewhat distressed. She had never violated curfew and was ruminating over the punishment that her parents might mete out to her for her infraction. Her brother had returned home nearly two hours earlier and was already sleeping. Jennie confessed the truth to parents, anticipating that she would not be believed. But to her surprise, her mother accepted her explanation. She knew that she wouldn't have intentionally avoided going to the game. But her reprieve was conditional upon one promise: she was to tell no one about her UFO sighting or lost time.

The UFO encounter and lost time, despite its perplexing elements, quickly vanished from Jennie's memory. Then one day nearly 40 years later, her mother brought it up in passing conversation. It came flooding back into her memory with emotional intensity.

Years later, I facilitated Jennie's recall of her missing-time event through hypnosis. She spoke of observing a rapidly descending, lighted craft that she thought was a helicopter. It hovered over the passenger side of the car and the engine died. Her friend was frantically attempting to restart the vehicle, while Jennie was chiding him with the news that it was a UFO. He began to exclaim that she was crazy—seconds before she was floated out the car window into the teardrop-shaped craft. It was very swift. On the craft, she came face-to-face with two gray non-humans that whisked her away to a larger craft. Feeling distressed, Jennie informed me that she wasn't prepared to access more detailed memories of her experience on the larger craft. Being sensitive to Jennie's need for emotional well-being, I suggested that she could move forward until she found herself back in the car. She was then able to recall the after-events and her panic about arriving home at nearly 11 p.m. on a school night in greater detail. Her testimony was consistent with her conscious recall.

As Jennie began to understand and accept her experiences, she realized that she had a long history of using denial as a coping mechanism to squash down her abduction memories. She had attempted to convince herself that the source of her intrusive flashbacks was linked to her earlier hypnosis sessions. In doing so, she attempted to forget the fact that witnesses had observed UFOs outside her home, additional family members shared her memories, and she had a missing-time event. Once she accepted this revelation, she realized that her denial had been a destructive psychological mechanism put in place because her truth was socially unacceptable.

After speaking with her family members, she began to realize that the glowing light orbs seen in her childhood home and observed by her parents and siblings were somehow related to her abduction memories. Doors opened and closed seemingly on their own, and household items left their position on shelves and flew across the room. Her teenage years were filled with sporadic paranormal activity that had not been apparent throughout her early childhood.

The Marden-Stoner study shed some light upon this question. Of the abduction experiencers, 88 percent reported the presence of psi phenomena such as glowing light orbs that rapidly expand or pop like a bubble into Grey extraterrestrials. Poltergeist activity, such as household items flying through the air, pictures flying off walls, lights turning off and on, windows and doors opening and closing, and electrical appliances operating on their own, even when unplugged, was also prevalent. Whereas, the members of the control group that reported paranormal activities in their homes, mentioned ghosts, shadow people, spirits, mist clouds, strange sounds, strange odors, and cold spots. This needs additional investigation to ascertain that the two groups are observing distinctly different phenomena. Until then, the jury is still out.

Jennie has the sense that the ETs are capable of producing many of the effects that we associate with the spirit world, but are related to ET science rather than disembodied spirits. She can't explain how she "knows" this, but she seems to possess knowledge that ETs can insert their consciousness into a ball of light in order not to frighten humans. This is a preventive measure, says Jennie, because human fear leads to hostility and the ETs find human emotions difficult to deal with. It permits them to monitor their human subjects with the least amount of apparent intervention possible. She also suspects that the process of transforming the physical human body into another dimensional state by increasing its vibrational frequency, then back to the physical for processing on the ET craft, and back to a higher vibrational frequency to be returned to a natural human environment at a lower vibrational frequency creates an electromagnetic energy discharge that causes poltergeist activity.

This aspect of alien abduction is not well understood and has been ignored by most abduction researchers, probably because we are most comfortable with the collection and study of tangible evidence. It clearly lies outside the tenets of Western scientific thought. I only began to study this phenomenon recently, when it became overwhelmingly clear to me that ignoring some of the evidence in favor of more scientifically acceptable evidence is scientifically dishonest: 88 percent is a highly significant statistic. Whereas it would be easy to summarily dismiss these phenomena as being psychologically generated, I have chosen to take the difficult route of attempting to find answers to the questions that lie outside the comfort zone of currently accepted scientific paradigms. We are not there yet, but I believe that abduction researchers such as myself who can impart knowledge of the alien abduction phenomenon to the brilliant theoretical physicists who have bravely stepped forward to explore the unknown are on the frontier of understanding a new science that might possibly alter our current scientific paradigms. Their brave exploration into the unknown will someday increase our understanding of this very perplexing enigma.

Abductions Resume

How does one cope with living between two lives? One life, by all appearances, is mainstream and filled with family, friends, community, and socially acceptable behaviors. The other secret life is dominated by an alien presence that intercedes sporadically, yet never leaves the forefront of one's mind. It is a difficult path to tread upon. Yet it is a course that Jennie has learned to maneuver throughout her teenage years and her adult life.

Jennie left her childhood home feeling hopeful that life would return to normal and was relieved when the intruders that had inserted themselves into her teenage years did not make their presence known in her college dormitory. She was grateful for the years of peace and the sense of normality that left her feeling grounded and comfortable. There were no more objects leaving shelves or being hurled through the air, no more floating orbs. Her life was filled with academic studies, in which she excelled, and college spectator sports—a chance to spend time with friends cutting loose from the pressures of mountains of homework. After graduating, Jennie landed a job as a teacher at an upstate New Hampshire high school, near the ski slopes that she loved to spend winter weekends coursing down. She shared a new apartment on the outskirts of town with a roommate.

The four-year abduction hiatus that had delivered a feeling of serenity to Jennie's life was about to end on the night that she returned home from a part-time second job to find her neighbors excitedly discussing their close encounter with a UFO that had hovered low near Jennie's bedroom window. The next morning, haunting memories of a nocturnal intrusion flooded her consciousness. Her roommate was spooked by this weird activity and soon moved to another state, but Jennie had nowhere to run to. She knew that her nocturnal visitors would find her regardless of where she laid her head. The fear of falling asleep returned like a dark cloud settling upon the valley. Intrusive memories pierced her waking hours, creating an uneasy feeling of insecurity. She knew that this was beyond coping in isolation, so she picked up the phone and called my aunt Betty Hill. She and Betty met and a referral was made to Dr. James Harder, the director of research for the now defunct Aerial Phenomena Research Organization. She worked with him for a time under the condition of confidentiality.

She had already met Tom, the man that would become her first husband, a real estate developer and respected business man. A few months later, she moved into his comfortable mountain chalet. It was situated outside of town on a 4-acre tract of land in a quiet country setting. There was only one neighbor nearby.

For a time, Jennie's nights were uneventful, at least as far as she could remember. But several months later, she awoke with an unsettling memory of alien intervention into her life. She and Tom had retired early that night and quickly fell into a deep sleep. Jennie awoke in the middle of the night to find that Tom was no longer in their bed. At first, she assumed that he had risen to use the bathroom and would return momentarily, so she lay awake waiting for him.

After what seemed to Jennie like a very long time, he appeared at the bedroom door flanked on each side by two figures. He said that he'd been outside and as he slipped into bed, his icy torso brushed against her warm body. Someone made her understand that it had not been necessary to take her that night. She only needed to be seen for a minor adjustment.

Her eyes fell upon three diminutive figures now with eyes that glistened like cat's eyes in the darkness. She was rolled onto her abdomen, but clung to Tom's frigid form. He steadied her as a sudden wave of terror began to course through every synapse of her rigid body. Next came the sensation of what seemed like a cold, hard instrument pressing against the upper portion of her spine. Suddenly, she began to feel nauseated, as images whirled through her mind like a movie reel on high speed. (This is a common element in abduction experiences.) Jennie recalled nothing more from that night but awoke the next morning feeling unsettled.

In the morning light and with trepidation, Jennie told Tom about the frightening dream she remembered from the night before. Although she had experienced it as real, she felt compelled to deny its reality to even those closest to her. Her hope that it had only been a nocturnal fantasy was shattered when Tom confessed his vague memory of the event. The suspicion that it was real dealt a second blow to Jennie when she lifted the sheet and her eyes fell upon mud and bits of vegetative matter beneath his feet. Jennie's blood ran cold. Quickly she stripped the bed and dashed for the laundry room, feeling compelled to destroy the evidence. For Jennie, the memory refused to fade away. It played over and over again in her thoughts, adding a new layer of mystery to her life.

Jennie and Tom were married that summer, and several months later decided to add a new member to their family. They attempted to conceive a child, but after months of trying, Jennie was still not pregnant. Her medical records indicate that although Jenny did not menstruate, she was ovulating. She and Tom would have a childless marriage unless they adopted. It was a major disappointment, but one that she resigned herself to accept.

During this timeframe, Jennie experienced several "visitor" encounters which she recalled only as haunting dreams. Then one night, when Tom was out of town on business, she had a very strong sensation that the non-human entities who'd been visiting her for years were nearby. Something like a telepathic message told her that she was pregnant, but there was a problem with the fetus that had to be corrected. It came as a strong sensation in her head that left her feeling frightened.

Jennie was fearful of spending the night alone and vulnerable. She resigned herself to the idea that by remaining awake throughout the night, she would be able to protect herself from being taken. She feared that the entities were tricking her into the belief that they intended to help her, when in reality they intended to remove the fetus from her body. She dressed in her flannel nightgown and sat upright on her bed nervously reading a book, hyper vigilant to the sounds in her house, watching for movement, refusing to close her eyes. Suddenly, she heard activity and checked her clock. It was 2:05 a.m. and her heart was pounding.

As if only an instant had passed, the clock read 4:10. Jennie was filled with haunting memories of finding herself in a strange room where she observed aquarium-like cylindrical tanks, each containing a fetus in a kind of amniotic fluid.[1] Some were fully formed, whereas others were very tiny. One cylinder contained a tiny fetus that her ET escort took a special interest in. She now sensed that the entities were planning to remove the fetus that she was carrying and replace it with a genetically modified fetus they had produced from her ova. She was then led to an adjacent room and told to lie down on a table. Moments later, she lost consciousness.

Years later, Jennie requested my assistance in facilitating her full memory of the events that fateful night. She is guided back to the domed room with illuminated walls from her earlier memory. She states:

There is something that needs to be repaired. My escort pauses at the third one [cylindrical tube], down from the wall and seems pleased with that one. Another person comes into the room and is looking at it. They look at the different fetuses in the different tubes, and I think that they are selecting one. I think that the one that I have can't survive, and they have to replace it.

Jennie suspects that all of the tubes in this room are incubating human life harvested from her body, but she has no evidence of this. The tiny fetus that her escorts gaze upon is tiny, rounded, and not well formed. It appears to be little more than a month old fetus.

Moments later Jennie is led into an adjacent room with a curved wall and a single table attached to the floor on a pedestal. There is a team assembled in the room. I ask Jennie to describe the team and she replies:

There are four more, I think, besides my escort, and they're all taller. There aren't any little short ones there. My escort is by my head. At least one is taller than my escort. Three are the same as my escort and one almost seems female. That's strange.

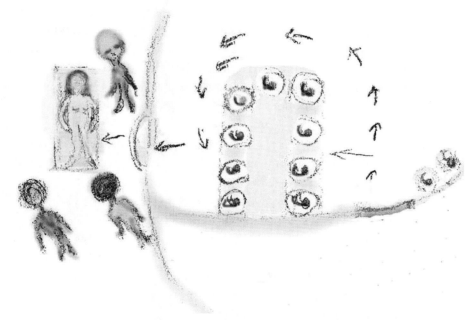

*Jennie's sketch of the room with fetuses in cylindrical tanks
and the examining room.*

I just sense the feminine. I am upset because I think that they
are taking my baby again. They have only said that there is
something wrong that they need to fix.

Jennie is beginning to exhibit signs of emotional distress. She
writhes and shudders. I offer calming suggestions to her and offer her
the opportunity to leave her memories behind. She calms and expresses
a desire to continue on. She continues:

I don't want them to do this. I'm crying and they say that this is
necessary. They have a long, thin instrument, and it is attached
to a tube. There was something on the end and then a frame
of some sort in the middle, and a tube. I think that they can
somehow penetrate the placenta and take the one and attach
the other one. This is my guess, but I'm only guessing.

When Jennie's procedure has been accomplished, she is escorted to
another room with a rectangular container that is filled with a viscous

fluid. There is a time lapse, and she has regained consciousness in the vat and has apparently been inhaling the substance without ill effect. Immersion in viscous fluid is a common but little known aspect of alien abduction. Experiencers have speculated that the gel might have a medicinal or nutritional value. There is a thicker fluid that might protect experiencers during transport into deep space, but all of this is purely speculative.

When she emerged from the fluid, it dried very quickly and didn't leave a visible residue. She was escorted into a hallway where she was rejoined by her escort. She recalled:

I'm with my escort. I think it was out in space because I somehow remember stars whizzing past. It is almost like I can see them all around me...like they were everywhere...like there was a big open area.

As she stood in the curved hallway with her escort approaching her final destination, three crew members emerged from a section of the craft that was beyond her visual range:

All of a sudden there is a hubbub. There was a sudden maneuver. I'm afraid that I'm losing my footing. I'm afraid that I'm going to fall down. But my guide tells me that it's okay. Everything is fine. Everything is fine—that I don't have to worry about that. Everything gets back on course again. They seemed distressed, as if they had an urgent matter on their hands. And we were safe, but they seemed concerned. If we had been destroyed, I would simply have disappeared off the face of the Earth, and no one would ever know what had happened to me. But we were safe now. We were coming in and I can see that we were coming up to my road...coming lower and lower...seeing the ground below...seeing the lights of my house.

We're coming in over my street, and my house isn't far from there. They come in over by my house. I am just transferred. A transfer takes place. I am there and he takes me down. It reminds me of a light beam in a way. It's like a shaft only there are walls. There seem to be walls on it and there's motion inside. Then I am returned to my bed. And he impresses a message upon my mind. It is very important that I drink of the stream.

I hadn't been asleep that night. When they took me I was awake, and when they returned me I was still awake. I looked at my clock and it's almost 4:10. I hope that I can sleep, but I don't think that I'll be able to, because I was so curious about all of this. I'm trying to figure out what "drink of the stream" means. Do they want me to go out to the brook and drink the water? I can't drink of the stream. But then I realize that he must be telling me to drink water...to take in fluids. I think that I need to cleanse my system. I think there has been a transfer, and they think that I should cleanse my system by drinking plenty of fluid.

Jennie advised me that she felt extremely fatigued that morning and spent most of her time in bed after calling in sick. She made an appointment with her physician for a pregnancy test, and to her delight, discovered that she was pregnant. This confirmed in her mind that her experience was real. Eight months later, she delivered a boy. He was a normal, healthy newborn, who in every respect displayed the physical characteristics of his mother and father. Jennie was convinced that her ET visitors had given her the one thing that she wanted most: a child.

I then brought Jennie's hypnosis session to a close and offered post-hypnotic suggestions that gave her permission to forget anything that she didn't want to remember. She emerged from hypnosis feeling relaxed and at ease.

Was it only a dream that she embellished during hypnosis? Had she fallen asleep reading her book with lights glaring throughout her house? We discussed the possibility, but Jennie rejected it. She had acquired new knowledge. She somehow "knew" that these beings were not genetically compatible with humans, but were able to splice their DNA onto a human chromosome in order to create a human form that possessed the characteristics that they found desirable. Likewise, they were able to splice a partial human DNA sequence onto their chromosome in order to experience a wider range of emotions—ones that they had either lost or never had. It was a segment of their experimental program with a species unlike themselves—a primitive people who are sharply individualistic, yet can express great compassion for others—sometimes greedy and violent, but also generous and loving.

In my role as an investigator, I was tasked with the responsibility of entertaining the idea that there might be a viable prosaic explanation for Jennie's memories. Her physical evidence was circumstantial at best and had been destroyed years earlier. I had to consider whether or not Jennie's dreams represented wish fulfillment. Psychological literature is filled with accounts of women who cannot conceive developing a false pregnancy in order to fulfill a psychological need. Jennie had wanted desperately to conceive a child and might have dreamed of benevolent ETs carrying out her wish. The cylindrical gestation tanks could have represented the amniotic fluid in a pregnant mother's womb. The gel-like substance that she recalled being removed from could represent a distant memory of her own birth. The sudden maneuver that placed them in a momentary tenuous position could have represented her fear of losing the pregnancy that she hoped for. But strange as it seems, similar occurrences are widely reported among abduction experiencers.

Well-known abduction researchers such as the late Budd Hopkins, David Jacobs, and Barbara Lamb have reported similar information. Beginning in the mid- to late 1980s, "missing fetus syndrome" emerged in UFO abduction literature and was hotly debated among researchers.[2] Although the phenomenon has been widely reported, no one has ever submitted medical records proving beyond a reasonable doubt that it is real. I wondered if Jennie had been exposed to media on this topic or if her dream was a manifestation of a collective unconscious that played out in women's dreams as wish fulfillment. It was interesting to me that her event contained more detailed information than had ever been included in published accounts of this phenomenon. In addition to this, she produced a typed account of her experience, written not long after it occurred, before there had been publicity about "missing fetus syndrome."

Whether or not Jennie's recall under hypnosis was fantasy or reality, she became less fearful and more settled after her session. She said that gaining access to her memories of the event made all the difference in the world. Years of anxiety melted away. She realized that the most frightening aspect of her abduction experience was her fear of the unknown. Prior to this, she had viewed herself as a victim, but now her perspective had changed.

Jennie's escort.

As Jennie moved forward in developing greater insight into her lifetime of contact experiences, she decided to explore another perplexing
encounter that occurred shortly after the birth of her son, Aiden. It was
the holiday season, and she and Tom had flown to North Carolina to
spend Christmas with his parents at their seasonal residence.

Jennie and Tom had fallen fast asleep in the guestroom with tiny
Aiden resting in a bassinet positioned against a wall near the foot of
the bed. She recalled being roused by Tom in the middle of the night

and instructed to pick up Aiden and follow him outside. She didn't want to go, but soon found herself outside in the company of her familiar Grey escort on her in-law's lawn. The stiff blades of grass were stinging her feet, so her familiar escort floated her a few inches above the ground. Fearing that she might drop Aiden, she passed him to Tom for safe keeping. A craft had landed at the bottom of a small embankment that led to a private pond. It was as long as a bus and rounded.

A familiar figure—one that she didn't like— was standing at the top of the ramp. She walked toward him, and Tom relinquished their infant son to two waiting entities. Jennie insisted upon accompanying Aiden to the examining room, but was informed that it would not be possible. In protest, she screamed and cried, but to no avail. In response, he communicated telepathically, "Do something to shut this one up." Jennie stated, "It's like he didn't even think of me as being human. It's like he thinks that I'm not fully human or something. It was like he didn't like humans. Or maybe he didn't like humans who were expressing the fearful emotions that were raging out of me." She continued:

> They took me...I don't know where. Tom disappeared too. They took me around to the left-hand side. It was like a dark little alcove and the ceiling was very low. It was only high enough for them to stand in. I had to bend down a little bit, so I wouldn't hit my head on the ceiling. [Jennie is 5'4".] There was just a table. It was kind of dark. I didn't see any light, but there was light reflecting in there from the outside.

One Grey entity was positioned by her feet and another by her head. At least one more stood by her lower side. (Abduction experiencers have consistently reported to me that the escort always stands by his or her head and the examiner stands by the feet. There are often others who serve as assistants who are shorter in stature.)

She recalled that a very painful procedure was performed on her, possibly as punishment for her noncompliant behavior. She had the sensation that an electrical current was passing though her shaking and vibrating body, causing her to burn and tingle. When the tingling subsided, she received the telepathic message that they were attempting to heal a physiological problem. She realized that it involved her ovaries, because she felt a painful burning sensation for the next several days. She was undecided whether she should be grateful to her captors for healing her, or feeling suspicious that they had intentionally harmed her as punishment for her bad behavior.

Soon Jennie was released and Aiden was brought down the hallway and placed in her arms. She was escorted down the ramp and met Tom. It that moment, she realized that she and Tom's memories were being manipulated. They were led to believe that we were looking at a bus or a motor home; not a landed alien craft. A conversation ensued about the attractive travel vehicle as she and Tom were guided back to the house.

Again, I had to consider the possibility that Jennie's memory was only a dream, caused by her anxiety over traveling with an infant. When I inquired about this possibility, she quickly added an additional piece of information by stating that the following morning, her mother-in-law asked why she and Tom had been outside during the night. She'd heard what sounded like Jennie weeping and Tom's voice outside her bedroom window. Jennie checked the front door and discovered that, although Tom's mother checked the deadbolt each night before she went to bed, it had mysteriously been unlocked. Everyone denied knowledge of how it had occurred.

The experience at her in-laws' house left Jennie feeling unnerved for a while. The fact that her infant was taken from her made her realize that this was an intergenerational family affair. She began to wonder where Tom fit into all of this, especially because he seemed to be acting as their agent. But she tried her hardest to push down her bizarre memories and carry on as usual. It worked for a while. But the nagging feeling that there might be more to the story left her feeling perplexed. She felt that she had a right to know the secrets that her visitors had been hiding from her.

As a UFO abduction researcher, I can only state that there has been a high incidence of electric-shock scenarios reported to me by abduction experiencers. I do not know why this is occurring. The feedback that I've received indicates that the ETs promote the idea that it is for the human's benefit. Yet there is an overriding feeling of distrust by abductees toward their captors, especially when the person has been subjected to medical and emotional experiments.

Two years after their first child was born, Jennie and Tom welcomed their second child, a daughter, into their home. They had enjoyed a much needed reprieve from the unwelcome intrusions that came in the night and hoped that it would continue, but all of that changed two months after Sarah's birth. Tom was out of town on business and planned to spend the night in a hotel and return home the next day. Early in the evening, Jennie had tucked 2-year-old Aiden into his crib in the nursery at the top of the stairs. Shortly thereafter, two friends arrived to enjoy an evening of roast duckling and quiet conversation. Her guests left at 11 p.m. and she retired to her bedroom with her infant daughter.

She carefully placed Sarah into her bassinette and covered her with a warm quilt, and then slipped into her nearby queen-sized bed. The room was cool, so she turned the dial on her electric blanket to a higher setting and quickly drifted off to sleep.

Jennie awoke at 2:10 a.m. feeling uncomfortably warm. She rose to use the bathroom and rehydrate with a tall glass of ice cold water. Sarah had begun to stir in her bassinette, so Jennie prepared her bottle and semi-reclined on top of the blankets on Tom's side of the bed, while she waited for the blanket on her side to cool. The table lamp cast soft, ambient light into the room as she lay facing her tiny daughter's bassinette.

Sarah's rhythmic breathing, interrupted by fitful squeaks, signaled that she would soon awaken. She entertained the idea of waking her while she was still fully alert. But in the next instant, before she could walk to the bassinette, a horrifying intervention occurred.

Without warning, some kind of energetic force flipped her body face down and in two swift movements zipped her across the bed, feet first. She is certain that she wasn't dragged, but was elevated slightly above the bed's surface. Her senses heightened as terror set in. Body trembling, she listened for the presence of intruders.

Face down and too frightened to move, she realized that only her head, torso, and thighs were on the bed. Her knees, calves, and feet extended beyond the precipice. Gripped by terror, she attempted to turn her head, to spring up from the bed, to rescue her infant daughter and flee from the terrible force that was holding her captive. But she couldn't. With all of the courage that she could muster, Jennie plead, "Leave me alone." It was barely intelligible. She's not certain if she was too frightened to move or paralyzed, but a sluggish tongue inside a nearly immobile jaw made her utterance nearly impossible. Too frightened to turn her head, she resorted to the only senses that were still functioning.

She felt a presence that seemed like two entities and heard a low buzzing sound much like that emitted from a bumblebee's nest. She could hear her infant daughter whimpering and stirring in her bassinette, but she was not able to move or respond to her needs.

Then suddenly, as if only a terrifying minute had passed, the paralyzing force released her, and once again her muscles began to function properly. But now she lay face down in a third location on the bed, on what had become a cool electric blanket. This was not a typical sleeping position for Jennie. She always slept on her back or side. She was not a restless sleeper, nor did she suffer from sleep disturbances or nightmares. She had never had this kind of experience before.

Still in possession of her faculties, she attempted to rationalize an explanation for her terrifying experience. But she couldn't find one. I had to weigh sleep paralysis, a prosaic explanation, against the possibility that Jennie had experienced another alien intervention.

Sleep paralysis is related to REM sleep, but is a different phenomenon. It can occur just before falling asleep or waking up. You will have conscious awareness of your surroundings but not be able to move anything except your eyes. You might observe shadowy figures in your bedroom and your heart might pound, as a sense of fear jars you into wakefulness. About 30 to 40 percent of those queried by sleep study scientists report that they have experienced sleep paralysis. It is simply a sign that their bodies are not moving smoothly through the stages of sleep.

Hypnagogic (between waking and sleeping) and hypnopompic (between sleeping and waking) hallucinations occur when factors such as stress, extreme fatigue, or medications cause the part of the brain that distinguishes between conscious perceptions and internally generated perceptions to misfire. This results in internally generated visions, sounds, feelings, smells, or tastes. H/H (hypnagogic/hypnopompic) hallucination experiencers often see colored geometric shapes or parts of objects. Others might observe the full image of a person, monster, or animal. Sometimes lines or the outlines of figures are observed. Sensations of floating or flying are common, along with hallucinated buzzing sounds. H/H hallucinations can be frightening. The hallucinations can last from seconds to minutes and are usually accompanied by a brief period of sleep paralysis. They are experienced as being as real as real. (Jennie had reported buzzing sounds and the sense of rapid movement, two common characteristics of sleep paralysis.)

If we experience a combination of sleep paralysis and H/H hallucinations, we will suffer intense fear and wake up paralyzed, unable to move anything except our eyes, just as Jennie did. We might observe shadowy figures standing beside our beds or hovering overhead. If we attempt to cry out, we find, as Jennie did, that we can't utter more than a nondescript sound. We're locked inside paralyzed bodies, unable to speak or move, except for our eyes. Our hearts pound, and we strain to breathe as if there is a weight upon our chests. We are acutely aware of our surroundings. Shadows transform into frightening shadowy images and sounds intensify. We struggle to break free from our dreadful predicament, and within seconds we are fully awake.

When one considers the details of Jennie's frightening account of possible procurement by aliens, we realize that sleep paralysis is not a good explanation for her experience. Shadowy figures were not part of Jennie's account; nor did she feel a weight on her chest. Her body was in a new location, on the opposite side of the bed perpendicular to her normal sleep position, and face down in a third location. She had experienced a time lapse. Moments earlier it had been 2:10. She was certain that she hadn't drifted off into the early stages of sleep. She was anticipating Sarah's signal that it was time for her bottle. Then suddenly and without prosaic explanation, the hands on the alarm clock read 4:00. Nearly two hours had passed in a flash. It was as if she had jumped from one moment in time to another with no apparent interval.

Frightened and confused, Jennie gathered the fortitude to leave her bed. She inspected her house for a sign of disturbance, but found nothing that she could recall. Finally, she carried her wakeful daughter to her bed and held her close, as she attempted to relax and find solace in her knowledge that the ordeal was over and they had survived. But Jennie couldn't relax. She was trembling with fear that could only be eased by the protective presence of a friend or neighbor. She waited until she saw the light blink on in her neighbor's home and pleaded for him to come to her aid. Over the ensuing three days, she would learn more about her experience than she had ever hoped for.

Jennie's neighbor had been awake when her experience occurred and had observed a craft hovering over her home. He assured Jennie that he'd look for additional witnesses and spoke with a friend on the police force.

I requested Jennie's journal from the night in question. It outlined her memories from that night and added an important piece of information. She wrote, "In the morning I sought the comfort and support of [my neighbor]. We also reported the incident to [a friend on the police force]. When we began our investigation, my friend found a man who had walked by my house that night. He saw people by my house."

Hypnosis facilitated Jennie's recall of the events that followed her nocturnal visitation. Although she possessed conscious recall of the events, hypnosis sharpened her memory. I asked her to move ahead to the day following her event when she expelled what she suspected was an implant from her nasal cavity. She responded as follows:

Jennie: I'm thinking of a time that Tom came home the next day and we were bathing Aiden and I started coughing and coughing and something flew out of my nose. It was the strangest little seed and it had a little wire-like thing coming out of each end of it. And I said to Tom, I think this is connected to what happened to me last night. And I said I'm going to save it and send it to Jim Harder. And Tom said, "Let me see that." And he took it and he flushed it down the toilet. I'd been trying to collect evidence for Jim and this was evidence. He destroyed the evidence.

Kathleen: Did he make any comments about why the evidence needed to be destroyed?

J: He just said, "You don't need that." And I started laughing about it because I'm thinking that if the ETs are trying to find me, they'll have a problem because it's in the sewer system. [Laughs.]

K: Alright now. Take a look and see if there is anything else that you recall that you want to add.

J: No, I don't think so.

This ended Jennie's session. The eyewitness accounts of a UFO above Jennie's house and figures entering her home seem to preclude the sleep paralysis explanation. As in any skiing community, the population is transient. Nearly 20 years had passed by the time Jennie came to me with her story. I have not been able to locate her former neighbors or their friend on the police force. This was an exchange between friends and no police report was filed.

Only two years after the nocturnal visit that shook Jennie to the bone, her husband lost his life in a tragic automobile accident. After Tom's death, Jennie and the children moved to southern New Hampshire and the security of her extended family. She hoped upon hope that her ET visitations would come to an end, even though she was near the childhood home where her uncanny experiences had begun. For a time, all remained quiet and she and the children were able to make a satisfactory transition into their new life. She eventually reunited with her childhood sweetheart, Doug, and they married. She and her children enjoyed several peaceful years and were able to put unpleasant memories behind them. But everything changed in January 1988. The intrusions into her life had caused her to become ill. Her children were traumatized by a disquieting force that suddenly disrupted their mundane family existence. She thought that she had somehow succeeded in persuading her unwanted visitors to leave her and her children alone. But then she realized that determination alone could not bring about change.

14

Serial Abductions

In an attempt to learn more about the nature of the intrusions into her life, Jennie and her second husband, Doug, decided to attend a UFO conference at the University of Nebraska, in Lincoln, from April 30 to May 2, 1994. Budd Hopkins would be lecturing on his research and Jennie hoped to speak to him personally, as well as a few other abduction researchers with less prominent names. She returned home with a little additional knowledge, but without the settled feeling that she had hoped for.

Their return trip was marred by severe thunderstorms wreaking havoc through America's heartland, and causing excessive delays in flights to the East. It was late in the evening when Doug pulled his Ford Bronco into their driveway. Feeling tired, Jennie went directly to the bedroom to unpack her suitcase and prepare for bed. She turned on her alarm clock and laid out her nightgown. Her thoughts were focused upon picking her children up from her parent's house in the morning, and seeing them off to school. Doug lingered behind in the family room, standing in front of the television set, taking in the late night news and weather report. Without explanation, their next immediate memory was of waking up in bed under bizarre circumstances.

The lights were still on, and the television was emitting a signal indicating that it was off the air. Jennie attempted to rise up out of bed, but found herself tucked in so tightly that she couldn't move. Doug had to free her from the clutches of her blankets. Both were astonished when they realized that they were fully dressed. Jennie was wearing her beige suit. Her pumps were still on her feet, and her jacket was fastened around her. Doug was still wearing his jeans and oxford shirt. They quickly undressed, and Jennie turned off the lights and television set. She was alarmed, but Doug persuaded her to disregard the perplexing situation, and return to bed. Soon they drifted off into a deep sleep. The following morning Jennie's memory was sharp, but her husband had only a vague remembrance of the unsettling event.

Years later, as Jennie recounted her memories of this bizarre occurrence, she reflected upon a similar event that had happened to another couple. She had learned about it at a MUFON meeting she had attended to learn more about UFOs and alien abduction. The MUFON member spoke of a couple that were possibly abducted during a vacation trip to New Hampshire's White Mountain region. Early in the evening, from the porch of their cottage, they had observed a UFO. Later that night, they were seated comfortably in the living room reminiscing about the day's events, when they noticed a bright light approaching. Their next memory was of waking up tucked so tightly into their bed that they had difficulty freeing themselves. They had simply lost several hours and had no memory of the events that had occurred between their observation of the light and waking up in bed.

This synchronicity of similar events has been reported to me by several abduction experiencers. I suspect that the ETs have a means of monitoring abductees' activities and creating similar scenarios, perhaps to let them know that they are being watched. In one of my cases, an abduction experiencer had awoken immediately upon being returned to her home following an abduction. She inspected her body for evidence that something more than a dream had occurred and found pressure marks in the shape of three long fingers on the inside surface of her lower legs. She immediately photographed the evidence and sent it to me.

I had told no one about the witness's evidence when, out of the blue, another abduction experiencer contacted me. The two did not know one other and were completely unfamiliar with the other's experiences. They came from different walks of life and resided in different states. The second experiencer informed me that she had been returned to her bed with three long, finger-shaped pressure marks on both of her inner calves. Both experiencers deny that they have visited alien abductee chat rooms or have read about this phenomenon. Since then, I have received additional reports from others.

One has to maintain a healthy level of skepticism in such cases, because some people are motivated to create hoaxes. I keep an open mind and don't reveal any evidence that I've received to the public until I have acquired supporting evidence from additional witnesses, nor do I ask witnesses if they have experienced similar events. I work quietly and cautiously, recording data and cataloguing evidence. I am continuing to catalogue more evidence of this occurrence. It could indicate that some female abduction experiencers have had their legs forcibly parted for what I suspect is a gynecological procedure.

Several abduction experiencers have photographed fresh scoop marks on their bodies immediately after they have been returned from what they remember as an abduction experience. They exhibit the characteristics of punch-hole biopsy. The 1/4 inch circle appears to have been cleanly cored out of the witness's flesh. As it begins to heal, a red dot appears in the center of the wound, suggesting that it might be deeper than the exterior circumference. The experiencer reports that he/she became aware of the flesh wound upon awakening, but did not have it prior to retiring for the night. These marks do not exhibit the earmarks of an insect bite. (Denise described this procedure in detail and carries the scar.)

Some abduction experiencers have reported that they have been returned from an abduction event dressed in someone else's clothing. Sometimes a man is returned wearing a woman's nightgown, as in the Stan Romanek case,[1] or a woman is dressed in someone else's nightgown. Pierced earrings are sometimes inserted backward and jewelry is sometimes missing. Nearly a dozen years ago, I found my aunt Betty Hill exhausted and in a quandary. She had retired for the night dressed in her red, plaid, flannel nightgown, but awoke without it. It had simply vanished and was never found. She complained that she felt as if she hadn't slept. When I entered her bedroom I noticed that an unfamiliar tee shirt lay neatly over the back of her chair. Betty believed that her 1961 abduction was a onetime event, but this was very perplexing. The plot got thicker when I attended MUFON's 35th Annual Symposium in Denver.

Deborah Lindemann, a certified and registered clinical hypnotherapist, presented a lecture on Stan Romanek's extraordinary ongoing abduction experiences. I was in the audience listening attentively, when she spoke of a baffling experience. Stan had gone to bed wearing a tee shirt and woke up dressed in a woman's red plaid flannel nightgown. I was stunned! Were Betty and Stan abducted on the same night and returned to their respective homes in the other's night clothes? I spoke briefly about it with Stan and decided to research the possibility. I couldn't find enough evidence to draw a conclusion, so it remained mere speculation.

My search was delayed because my aunt was terminally ill and required my constant care. Betty passed away in October 2004, and I was busy completing the book about her life, *Captured! The Betty and Barney Hill UFO Experience.* It wasn't until 2009 that I saw Stan Romanek again. We had been invited to speak at the Mysteries of the Universe conference in Kansas City, and the conference organizer, Margie Kay, asked us to arrive a day early. This gave us the rare opportunity to meet for casual conversation. Stan's wife, Lisa, and I attempted to pin down the dates when the nightgown incidents occurred and discovered that Stan's nightgown couldn't possibly have belonged to Betty Hill. The dates were wrong. It was just a weird coincidence, yet an intriguing one.

Household items sometimes go missing in experiencer's homes and are returned in a manner that suggests the aliens want to make their presence known. One experiencer reported to me that she kept a camera on her nightstand hoping to snap a photograph of her intruders. One morning she awoke with memories of a nocturnal intrusion and her camera was missing. She and her family searched their home for the camera to no avail. Several days later, the camera appeared atop a pile of laundry situated next to the washer and dryer. Family members denied putting it there. Seemingly, there is no prosaic explanation for this event, as the witness is not a sleepwalker and family members have a mutually respectful and open relationship.

Another commonality among experiencers is their propensity to be truly perplexed by their memories of nocturnal visitation. They play them over and over again in their minds, attempting to make sense of them. Memories of lying on a hard surface with non-humans conducting procedures on their immobile bodies occupy their minds. Most receive messages meant to calm them and inform them that they are performing an important function. Some are enlightened with information that they are extraterrestrial beings that have been created by the ETs in human form in order to experience life on planet Earth. They were born to biological parents from their own genetically modified DNA. The ET's life force entered the human baby prior to birth. I know that some of this seems farfetched, especially to readers that embrace Western scientific materialism. But the reports are many.

Jennie had all of the characteristics of an abduction experiencer who was obsessed with questions pertaining to her encounters. She found herself replaying her intrusive memories over and over again in her thoughts. Her attempts to lead a normal life and to refocus her thoughts in a constructive manner were thwarted by her natural curiosity. She knew that obsessing upon one's abduction memories can be counterproductive and energy draining, especially when there is emotional anxiety. But try as she may, she couldn't forget. It was the first thing that entered her mind when she woke up in the morning and the last thing she thought about as she drifted off to sleep at night.

She feared for her children's safety, but she couldn't force herself to broach the subject with them. Aiden and Sarah were sleeping with weapons under their mattresses. There was evidence that they were lying awake throughout the night and slumbering only as the sun was rising. Both were exhausted in the morning and experienced difficulty preparing for school, even though they had formerly been well-rested, high achievers. But despite the mounting obstacles, they both graduated from high school on time.

In their late teens, both had frank conversations with Jennie about their own abduction memories. They had been scared by their intrusive nocturnal visitations, and had finally gathered the courage to speak to their mother face-to-face. It was a conversation that she had avoided when they were younger, because she hadn't wanted them to be thought of as odd or eccentric by their classmates. The transition from adolescence to adulthood is difficult enough without adding extra baggage to it. But the children had reached their late teens and it was time for a conversation.

Jennie began by advising them that whether or not their memories were dreams or reality, no physical harm had befallen them. If indeed they had been visited by astronauts from a distant planet, they should be perceived as scientists attempting to learn more about life on Earth. If their intention had been to harm the Henderson family, they would already have done so. But instead they had shown good intentions by partially erasing their conscious recall. Finally, they were able to put their concerns behind them and to move on in a positive manner. She encouraged them to focus upon their family, friends, education, and career goals, and to avoid obsessing upon life's mysteries, particularly those pertaining to alien abduction.

A small percentage of abductees have learned to view their experiences in a positive light. Often their early abductions were terrifying, but somewhere along the way they realized that their visitors do not wish to harm them. They believe they are merely sentient beings from another solar system or dimension who are communicating with Earthlings and perhaps extracting human DNA for their studies. They voice altruistic intentions through telepathic communication. Sometimes they co-opt their chosen human to assist them with the procurement and herding of other humans. Often they impart special knowledge to the "experiencers." This understanding and acceptance might have been facilitated through regressive hypnosis, enculturation, or conscious recall of a special relationship.

As Jennie worked to lose her fear related to her abduction experiences, her anxiety diminished. Although a home security system seems ineffective in preventing human procurement, it served as a psychological safety net for her. She found that she could easily fall asleep and remain asleep throughout the night. Occasionally she awoke with inexplicable bruises and pain in areas that seemed to have an anomalous source.

Not long ago, she discovered three long bruises on her right hip that resembled long finger prints and a scoop mark on her left arm above her elbow. Prior to finding these wounds, she had informed me that her abduction experiences had possibly ceased. That is, until one morning she awoke with memories of lying on a table in an examining room. She consciously recalled that a tall, thin, insectoid figure was busily working on her to remove a scoop-like flesh sample. As the wound healed, the center remained redder than the circumference.

Jennie described the insectoid as approximately 6 feet tall and extremely thin, with very large eyes and a tiny mouth at its jaw line. At least three of its possibly four fingers are very long and thin, with knobby joints meeting a small palm. She felt that it was kind and empathetic and left her with a message to carry to me. Jennie wrote to me that he conveyed the following information to her. He stated, "Many of the things that we think and others say about us and our program are not true. There is too much speculation and not enough facts." Jennie stated that she had a strong sensation that she possesses far more information than she is able to presently recall and that it will be unlocked at a later date, when the time is right. Many abduction experiencers have delivered the same message to me.

She recalls being taken by only the Greys and the Insectoids, who she reports work together cooperatively. Other abduction experiencers have reported that they received unkind treatment by an alien species known at the Reptilians. Their agenda appears to focus upon human reproduction and their interest in engaging in sexual intercourse with humans and in observing humans engaging in sexual intercourse. Jennie denies having contact with this negative race.

Jennie recently wrote to me that nearly seven months ago, she was jolted awake by pain in her chest area so intense, that she wondered if she was having a heart attack. Her upper right thigh was also excruciatingly painful and there were isolated pockets of pain distributed throughout her body. Trying not to panic, she opened her eyes to discover that she was on an examining table surrounded by three Grey beings. A strong pins and needles sensation was coursing through the outer surface of her entire body. Her escort showed her an image of her body, indicating the areas of pain and the energy that had enveloped her. The electric shock sensation lasted for several minutes followed by a sudden loss of time. When she awoke the following morning, she felt completely well. Her chronic joint pain had disappeared and she had more energy than she had experienced in years. Her good health has continued, although her small aches and pains from aging are present on a daily basis. Her energy level remains higher than it has been since 1988, and she has not experienced a relapse of CFIDS.

The most significant transformation in Jennie came when she ceased viewing herself as a victim and attempted to search for answers. She has, in the not too distant past, recovered from the trauma directly related to her abduction experiences. Today her quest for knowledge pertaining to the alien agenda is shared with several experiencers from around the world. All have acquired similar knowledge and view their experiences as non-threatening and friendly. Although her non-human visitors continue, from time to time, to insert themselves into her life, she is grateful for the knowledge that she is acquiring.

15

Fantasy or Reality?

My purpose in telling Jennie's story is neither to confirm nor deny the physical reality of her UFO abduction experiences. Like the majority of abduction experiencers, she hasn't handed over undeniable evidence that can be examined in a laboratory or exhibited in a museum. Instead, she has presented a different type of acceptable evidence—eyewitness testimony. She was not alone. Witnesses observed a UFO in close proximity to her home at the same time that she recalled being in an alien environment. Her husband stated that he is aware of odd occurrences in their home that seem to have no prosaic explanation. Her parents confirmed that Jennie experienced missing time as a teenager, and her mother stated that she too believes she has experienced alien abduction. In addition to this, several members of her extended family have had similar experiences.

Jennie permitted me to view her confidential medical records confirming that she was treated by a physician for injuries sustained during what her diaries indicate were three abduction experiences. She was actively treated for CFIDS during a period of several years. She has been in remission since April 2012, following what she perceived to be alien intervention. Time will tell if she has been healed.

Jennie completed the Marden-Stoner study. Not all participants answered every question. Some could not recall or simply did not respond to every question. Fractions were rounded off. Her responses are consistent with those submitted by 50 self-identified abduction experiencers. This positive correlation suggests that her experiences might be real. But her lack of physical evidence will never satisfy those who require a craft or an alien body with non-human DNA to accept the veridicality of her story. The following characteristics correlated positively with the self-identified abduction experiencers who participated in the "Marden-Stoner Commonalities Among Abduction Experiencers" study.

1. Jennie and 64 percent (32 of 50) of the participants are of the female sex. Nine of 25 (36 percent) participants in the non-experiencer group are women.

2. She and 79 percent of the 47 experiencers that answered the question believe they have had more than one abduction experience. Only 2 of the experiencer group reported one abduction only. 8 were not certain.

3. She and 76 percent (32 of 42) of the experiencers stated that they were not alone when they were taken. Three members of Jennie's family stated that they were abducted with her.

4. She had conscious recall for at least part of her abduction experience, as did 88 percent (44 of 50) of the experiencers in the study. Jennie is a rare experiencer in that she has conscious, continuous memories of some of her experiences. She also recalled it though dreams, like 56 percent of the participants in our study. She and 36 percent of the participants have entered into hypnosis. Hypnosis augmented Jennie's pre-existing memories.

5. She and 56 percent had conscious recall (not with hypnosis), of observing non-human entities prior to an abduction experience.

6. Witnesses reported that they observed a UFO near her house, vehicle, tent, etc. prior to or during their abduction. This was true of 43 percent of the experiencer group.

7. She and 67 percent (28 of 42) stated that they consciously recalled (not with hypnosis), the observation of an unconventional craft at less than 1,000 feet prior to an abduction experience.

8. She and 58 percent of the experiencer group (29 of 50) are aware of having been examined on an alien craft.

9. She and 68 percent of the experiencer group reported malfunctions of electrical equipment such as lights, digital watches, computers, etc. 32 percent of the control group reported similar malfunctions. Jennie has reported electrical anomalies, computer malfunctions, grocery store scanner malfunctions, and appliances blowing out. A strong electrical field was measured around her body after a reported abduction experience that was not present among others that participated in the test.

10. She and 88 percent (43 of 49) of the experiencer group have witnessed paranormal activity in their homes such as light orbs, objects that fly through the air, lights that turn off and on, doors opening and closing, etc. Of the 43 that answered in the affirmative, 22 stated that it began after their first abduction. 44 percent (11 of 25) of the non-experiencer group reported that they have witnessed paranormal activity in their homes, such as ghosts, shadow people, spirits, strange sounds, and variations in room temperature. Jennie has observed glowing light orbs in her home, an object flying through the air, doors opening and closing on their own, and shimmering iridescent clusters of varying sizes in her home.

11. She and 88 percent (44 of 50) of the experiencer group reported they have received telepathic messages from their ET visitors. 91 percent (30 of 33) stated that these messages were related to an abduction experience. 32 percent of the non-experiencer group (8 of 25) reported telepathic communication.

12. She and 50 percent (25 of 50) of the experiencer group reported that they have been given a gift of healing, at least briefly, following an abduction experience. Jennie's healing abilities were short lived and occurred immediately after an abduction. She believes that she was healed by her

non-human visitors during a visit in 2012 and has remained symptom free.

13. She and 72 percent (36 of 50) stated that they are more sensitive or intuitive than they were prior to the abduction.

14. She and 79 percent of those who responded (26 of 33) stated that they developed new psychic abilities after an abduction experience. (Two stated "maybe" and 15 were not able to answer the question)

15. On a daily basis, her mood is happy and/or without unusual highs or lows. This is true for the majority of participants in both groups. As a child, her mood was happy and without unusual highs or lows. (*Note: A larger percentage of the experiencer group (13) reported that they were sad as children. This was not true of the non-experiencer group (0). Note: Those who have traumatic memories of being abused by their adult caretakers or ETs are more likely to feel sad as adults and children.)

16. The majority of participants in the experiencer group reported that they used one or more coping mechanisms to deal with their anxiety pertaining to their experiences. Jennie used meditation, prayer, writing, reading, and keeping busy. (This is an open-ended question. Many stated that they found relief from meditation, writing, and talking with friends.)

17. Her emotional response to her abduction experiences is consistent with many other experiencers who stated that they felt extremely fatigued and unwell after being taken, angry about being taken against their will, and frightened when it occurred. As a daily coping mechanism to deal with any fear or anxiety due to her abduction experience, she has used meditation, relaxation, writing, and the support of others that she can speak with, without being judged.

18. She and 74 percent (37 of 50) of the experiencer group had difficulty falling asleep. She and 71 percent (35 of 49) of the experiencer group had difficulty staying asleep. This problem resolved for Jennie after she overcame her fear of abduction through education and hypnosis.

19. She has a medical diagnosis of chronic fatigue syndrome and reactivated mononucleosis. 38 percent (18 of 48) of the experiencer group has this diagnosis, although the prevalence among the general population is less than 1 percent for CFS. 2 additional experiencers state that they have the symptoms but no formal diagnosis. Jennie became disabled with this condition after her abduction in 1988 and had to take a leave of absence from work.

20. She and 83 percent (40 of 48) have awakened with unexplained marks on their bodies. Jennie has discovered burns, bruises consistent with finger marks, scoop marks, and rectal bruises on her body.

21. She and 52 percent (26 of 49) have awoken with a bloody nose and memories of an abduction experience. Only 20 percent (5 of 25) of the non-abduction experiencer group has awoken with a bloody nose.

22. She and 69 percent (22 of 32) have experienced gynecological problems that they suspect are related to their abduction experiences. Only 33 percent (3 of 9) of the female non-experiencer group reported experiencing gynecological problems. Jennie has experienced bleeding and bruising in the absence of sexual activity that her doctor cannot explain.

23. She developed light sensitivity following an abduction experience, like 28 of 50 experiencers. Jennie and the majority of participants stated that they had not developed more acute hearing, more allergies, or more fluctuations in mood.

24. She and 57 percent (26 of 46) of the experiencer group do not suffer from migraine headaches. 43 percent do, whereas only 8 percent of the non-experiencer group suffers from migraines. It is 10 to 12 percent among the general

population. Jennie reported having migraines after her 1988 abduction.

25. Like 63 percent (29 of 46) of the experiencer group, she did not notice skin rashes immediately after an abduction.

It is undeniable that Jennie exhibits nearly all of the characteristics that are common among UFO abduction experiencers. The prevalence of these commonalities among the abduction experiencer population is not widespread in the general population, as was indicated on the "Commonalities Among Non-Abduction Experiencers Questionnaire."

The question of paranormal activities in the homes of abduction experiencers has been reported throughout the history of UFO abduction research and investigation. Given its nature and our current adherence to the tenets of Western scientific materialism, it is not a topic that most UFO abduction researchers have been willing to examine seriously. To do so might result in the loss of one's reputation as a scientific researcher. For many years, I closed my eyes to this aspect of alien abduction, but the "Marden-Stoner Commonalities Among Abduction Experiencers" study" makes it abundantly clear that we can no longer sweep it under the rug: 88 percent of the respondents answered in the affirmative, stating that they have witnessed this activity in their homes. This does not mean that UFO abductions are an event related to spirits, angels, demons, astrals, or interdimensional beings. Most experiencers are convinced of its physicality. They can feel the non-human entity's skin and observe its body. They describe the craft's internal environment and equipment in a physical sense. They have viewed the craft close up while driving, hiking, or hunting, etc., and experienced missing time. Light orbs that rapidly expand into tangible non-human entities, transport through solid objects, and telepathic communication are some of the phenomena that cannot be explained by our current scientific laws. This suggests that these technologically advanced beings have discovered scientific principles that we have not yet discovered and do not understand.

Although physical evidence can be analyzed in laboratories, the paranormal aspects are best understood by theoretical physicists and parapsychologists. There are many things that we do not know about our world, including the characteristics of life in other dimensions and the feasibility of moving from one dimension to another. This work is best left to those who specialize in it.

Jennie's road is difficult to imagine for anyone that has not walked in her shoes and is impossible for many to accept. Some might suspect that she has long-standing delusions, even though her psychological tests are normal. Or they may question whether she has interpreted her dreams as real events, despite her documented missing time and the observation of UFOs in close proximity to her home by independent witnesses. The physiological evidence and her responses on the "Marden-Stoner Commonalities Among Abduction Experiencers" study add additional layers of support to the possibility that she might have been abducted repeatedly by non-human entities. But all of this must be weighed with a skeptical eye.

In my role as investigator-researcher, I am tasked with the responsibility of examining the evidence in an unbiased manner, while assisting Jennie in understanding the complexities of her situation. Without irrefutable evidence, I can neither confirm nor deny that her experiences are real. Each piece of evidence must be weighed and examined and prosaic explanations should be taken into consideration. As an experiencer advocate, I can offer support for the subjective reality of Jennie's experiences. She and thousands of others from around the world are reporting nearly identical intrusions into their lives by what they perceive as non-human entities. Crafts are observed and diminutive Grey beings with large craniums and penetrating eyes are observed assisting tall skeletal insectoid beings with large vertical eyes and a tiny mouth.[1] These beings impart telepathic messages of love and reassurance. Hundreds—if not thousands—of individuals report identical procedures performed in small, rounded rooms. The experiencer is visited throughout his or her lifetime. It seems too unbelievable to be objectively real. Yet if this is a psychological aberration, it is widespread, reaching across the world to nearly all races, cultures, religions, and socioeconomic groups.

• • • • • • • • • • • • •

16

Not Alone

Denise and Jennie are but two of dozens of individuals with whom I have spoken who share similar memories, some with less recall than others. Both women share memories of specific technology, medical conditions, psychological responses, and psi experiences that appear to relate directly to their abduction experiences. Denise's well-detailed conscious recall of some events, missing time with family members, and eyewitnesses to UFOs near her home add credence to her story. For Denise, hypnosis brought to the surface richly detailed memories of the craft, the beings, and the messages she received.

Jennie's conscious, continuous recall of the intrusions into her home and the events that occurred in an alien environment are unusual among experiencers. A post hypnotic suggestion brought forth memories that were previously repressed. Hypnosis merely augmented and added detail to her already existing memories. Taken together, her missing-time event, psychological tests, physiological evidence, and witnesses add credence to her story.

The final section of our book is devoted to others who believe they have been abducted. I have interviewed these witnesses, but have only done a preliminary investigation of their cases. Like the majority of experiencers, many have the earmarks of alien abduction. Some state that they observed a craft or non-human entities at close range and experienced missing time. Others recall nocturnal visitations dating back to childhood. Some remember their events in detail, whereas others have only fleeting memories. All have lived through an experience that to them defies prosaic explanation and their only explanation for it lies in extraterrestrial visitation.

One experiencer underwent something so profound that she feels she must tell it. At the same time, if she were to reveal her true identity, she and her family would risk having life as they know it shattered. For this reason, "D. Lynne Bishop" cannot step out of the shadows and reveal her true identity, but she is willing to share the information in her unpublished manuscript. It is brimming with vivid accounts of alien abduction, remembered both consciously and through hypnosis. Messages imparted to her by her alien visitors and her detailed account of alien abduction are nearly identical to—and sometimes verbatim yet not found elsewhere—those received by Denise and Jennie. Her story is so startling, yet confirmed by witnesses that it deserves to be told.

Lynne's experiences have been investigated under hypnosis by John Carpenter, MSW, LCSW, a clinical social worker from Missouri, well known in the UFO abduction field. In addition to this, she had a close relationship with the late Karla Turner, PhD, a former college professor, alien abduction experiencer, researcher, and advocate for abductees. Lucius Farish, the late editor of MUFON's news clipping service, knew Lynn personally and vouched for her honesty in a written document. Her story is lengthy, fascinating, compelling, and multifaceted, but due to space limitations we can tell only a tiny portion of it in this book.

Lynne's alien abduction history spans more than 50 years. It is multigenerational and includes her mother, sister, brother, husband, nieces and nephews. All have repeatedly been taken aboard a craft by non-human entities and subjected to intrusive medical procedures, without their consent. Lynne's earliest memory of alien abduction dates back to age 4. A year earlier, she, along with her mother and siblings, observed an erratically moving object with rotating lights that whooshed only 200 feet above their Houston, Texas, home. They were not the only witnesses. Additional observers inundated the phone lines at Ellington Air Force Base and the local newspaper office with inquiries about the UFO that was sighted overhead. When they finally were able to get through, they were informed that the military had nothing of the kind flying that night.

Lynne was 18 when she became aware for the first time that something unusual was occurring in her life and that of her family members. She and her mother were 2 hours into a 3-hour-long trip home after tending to personal business in one of Arkansas' large cities. Relaxed and enjoying each other's company, they had passed through a small town at the base of the Ozark Mountains and stopped at a road construction blasting site. Moving again, they were approaching the turn onto the highway that would lead them to their home. Suddenly and without warning, everything went totally blank. In what seemed like an uninterrupted sequence of events they found themselves on a totally new stretch of unfamiliar road, lined with large overhanging trees. Attempting to locate their position, Lynne's mother searched for a road sign. Almost immediately, Lynne screamed a warning that a car was rapidly approaching on a collision course with their vehicle, before it vanished. Then, suddenly and without explanation, they found themselves on the opposite side of town feeling uneasy and hypervigilant. Their next memory was of observing a silent, cigar-shaped, white or silver-colored craft that seemed to be pacing them. Lynne's mother, who was married to a lieutenant colonel in the Army, knew that this craft had no earthly origin. Finally, they were able to proceed along their route home, but their arrival added an additional layer of mystery to their day. More than an hour's time had simply vanished.

Nearly 20 years later, Lynne and her mother entered into hypnosis as a method of enhancing their memories of the close encounter and breaking through the wall of amnesia that had prevented them from discovering what had occurred during their period of missing time. In John Carpenter's office, Lynne and her mother discovered that they did indeed have a lot of rethinking to do about their UFO sighting and missing time event on that fateful day long ago.

Under regressive hypnosis, Lynne found herself inside the craft, encountering beings clothed in silver, skin-tight body suits with no defining line at the waist. Their bald, rounded, non-human heads were larger than ours, but perched upon a smaller neck. Their faces were flat on the bottom—like they were wearing masks. The forehead region bulged up and out. She described the remainder of their faces as "flat and narrowed down, very sharp" as if they were wearing helmets with a visor. No ears were visible. The creature's hands were "definitely not human."[1] She could see long fingers and an opposable thumb, but didn't think it had the same number of fingers as humans. Lynne's mother's description of the entities was nearly identical to hers.

In later sessions, Lynne described Grey entities whose facial expressions indicated emotion, although they lacked the range of emotions expressed by humans. She observed a taller entity working in concert with the shorter group who seemed more "Oriental-looking" in appearance. His head was more compact and his eyes were smaller and dark brown, not black. She found the wrinkles on his forehead reassuring, along with his thin lips and semi-human appearance. He was there to calm her, to let her know that he'd been with her "forever." He removed a red and black piece of tissue from her the size of the palm of her hand and approximately an inch thick. She described a kind of dentist's chair identical to the ones described by Denise and Jennie, and equipment that was comprised of a metallic robotic arm with two rods, identical to the one that Jennie observed during her fetus intervention procedure.

Lynne's memories of being captured and examined in an alien environment created an even more acute sense of hyper-vigilance within herself. Her odd dreams continued and she developed new emotional symptoms, such as fear of the dark, not wanting to be alone, lying awake between the hours of 1 and 3 a.m., and sleeping only 2 hours at a stretch. This is common among abduction experiencers and was true of Jennie after her first hypnosis session. The fear and anxiety experienced by those who endure the shock of realizing that they've been taken by a group of non-humans generally begins to subside after several hypnosis sessions.

Strange events continued to intercede, sporadically, in Lynne's life. Dreams of medical examinations aboard an alien craft, the harvesting of tissue samples, and baby presentations were interspersed throughout her adulthood. There were recurring physiological symptoms, such as unexplainable bruises and scoop marks carved into her flesh, and a fight-or-flight emotional response. All had no prosaic explanation. She remembered hearing high-pitched tones followed by a sudden silence that is known to precede an alien encounter. After her hypnosis sessions, she sometimes retained a conscious memory of being captured by Grey aliens. There were glimpses of lying on an examining table surrounded by non-human entities that performed medical procedures on her and engaged in non-verbal communication before she was returned to her former location.

In another hypnosis session, Lynne recalled that her family observed a craft landing in their yard. Some of the family members were "frozen" in limbo for a period of time while other family members were escorted out to the craft, and later returned. It happened time and time again and there was no recourse, no one who can make this family's experiences cease.

Later, she consciously recalled observing a craft in the yard and the subsequent observation of entities in her home. There were memories of being taken out to the craft by these aliens, but her memory was too hazy to fill in the details of her experience onboard the craft. Lynne underwent hypnosis to enhance her memory and realized that she was being escorted by two small Greys into a gray room with no doors or windows. Smaller entities assisted her onto a table. She could somehow "see" that she was pregnant. A different type of being, who was at least a foot taller than the others, entered the room. Lynn could no longer sense any communication, but she knew why she was there. Like Denise, she had something they wanted. When she was released, she was no longer pregnant.

Lynne wrote the following poignant statement about the impact of alien abduction upon her life:

> Yes, I have grown emotionally and spiritually. However, I attribute the growth to my inner resources; not to an alien creature whose interference in my life created turmoil. I would no more thank a devastating accident for occurring in my life, regardless of the growth caused by my survival of a traumatic event. We must learn to differentiate between outcome and catalyst, or we will forever run in fear as victims, or worship at the feet of a false god.
>
> I have no idea where these entities come from, whether they are extraterrestrial, interdimensional, time-travelers, or a form of earth life that has always existed side-by-side with humans. Perhaps all that really matters is that they are here, now, and we need to deal with them.

Whatever these aliens are, wherever they come from, can't we meet them, not as children, not as supplicants on our knees begging for an end to our ills, but instead on equal footing, standing eye-to-eye, as responsible adults?

Now, nearly 50 years after her first encounter, Lynne continues to experience nocturnal visitations. They involve not only her, but her husband and extended family. Her unpublished manuscript is brimming with vivid accounts of alien abduction, remembered both consciously and through hypnosis. It is information so startling, yet confirmed by witnesses that we feel compelled to include it in *The Alien Abduction Files*.

Our next account of alien intrusion begins somewhat differently than the first. The witnesses did not become aware of an alien intervention after observing an unconventional craft and experiencing missing time. They have memories of encountering non-human entities dating back to their early childhood. Audrey Hewins is an identical twin who grew up in a kind, nurturing, professional household. Early in her life she and her sister Debbie begged their parents not to put them to bed at night because the "bald men" were going to get them. They feared that diminutive entities with oversized craniums and black glistening eyes would take them somewhere and do things to them. They were so distressed by these memories that from age 5 on they began to keep notebooks filled with sketches of the bald men. When they were old enough to write, they filled pages in their diaries with detailed accounts of their unusual nocturnal visitations.[2]

When they were 14, their mother was shopping and saw an alien face on the cover of Whitley Strieber's book *Communion*. The most prominent feature was large, black, almond-shaped eyes, just like the ones that her daughters had been sketching for years. She discussed this uncanny similarity to her daughters and decided to take their diaries for safe keeping.

As the sisters grew older and moved from Ohio to Massachusetts, the beings began to emerge from their bedroom closet. They were a different type now that resembled humanoid reptiles. One time, both sisters felt they had been taken to an underground location and forced to engage in sexual relations with a very tall, broad Reptilian. They share memories of enduring similar unpleasant abduction experiences throughout their adult lives. Audrey stated:

There are reptile beings that I don't have such pleasant memories of. They are just mean. They have no sympathy...no feelings at all. They just come in and do whatever they want. Their vicious attacks are not enjoyable. I feel their energy and it's almost like they are sucking out my soul...like they're sucking the energy from you. It's a creepy feeling.

One Reptilian being entered Audrey's room and in a sci-fi type demon's voice said, "Why don't you come with me?" He was more than 6 feet tall and wearing a cape with a silken thread that had a metallic appearance when he moved under certain lights. When Audrey refused to accompany him, a light appeared above and to the right of her bed and he disappeared into a swirling area of it.

Another time she felt that she'd been raped in her bedroom by a good-looking man that suddenly turned into a green lizard-like reptile resembling Sleestak from the show "Land of the Lost." There was no sexual evidence that she'd been raped, but she had bruises in the shape of finger marks on her inner thighs and arms.

I had been investigating Audrey's Reptilian abduction report and knew that the preliminary results of our "ET Technology Survey" indicated that nearly 40 percent of the participants had reported contact with Reptilians. (This the second part of the "Marden-Stoner Commonalities Among Abduction Experiencers" study.) Almost without exception, reports of this kind are negative. These creatures purportedly arrive under the cover of darkness and inflict pain upon women and female children. They do not seem to have redeeming qualities, except in a tiny percentage of experiencers that consider them benevolent.

The evil sounding voice reported by Audrey caused me to wonder if somehow a demonic, rather than extraterrestrial, presence had entered her home, but I knew almost nothing about the subject. I had become sensitized to the possibility by Southern Conservative Christians, who have suggested to me that the only possible explanation for these events is a demonic presence. My inquiries to Audrey gave me an additional clue. At a young age, a neighborhood woman had drawn the twins into her occult world. Both stated they feel that they were taken by the dark forces when they were younger and have struggled to bring themselves into the light. Both women have sought religious intervention, but the road has been difficult. Not wanting to tread on unfamiliar ground and fearing the possibility that I might come face-to-face with something I couldn't handle, I made a referral to another researcher that specializes in spirit phenomena. Thus far, no firm conclusion has been established.

When I asked Audrey to present her most convincing evidence of extraterrestrial visitation to me, she spoke of an incident that occurred on January 3, 2007. It was late at night, she explained, and she was becoming nervous because she sensed "they" were coming. She described it as "like a panicky, inner anxiety—like a magnetic sensation—like I'm attracting something. It's hard to explain but I've been feeling that since I was a child when the Grey ones come."

Her journal notes that her visitations are most likely to occur during the new moon cycle—two days before and two days after—and on the full moon. The moon was full on January 4, 2007. She suspects that the reason for taking her on the new moon cycle is because she is ovulating and it is the best time for performing their reproductive experiments on her. She stated, "I remember being awoken on a table and they are scraping my left ovary. They put me asleep right away after that."

In another incident she was awake in her bedroom in the middle of the night when she felt a tingling sensation followed by muscle spasms. Soon her body stiffened with an all too familiar paralysis. She tried to fight it off, but she couldn't. Then she could only move her eyes. She described what happened next as follows:

> When my room filled with the light pale bluish light and the beings, I opened my eyes. The light shimmered and moved like a pool reflection on the ceiling. I wanted to see who they were. There was two smaller ones on each side of my bed and a taller one at the end. He was very familiar. I think he's always been there. The tall one was about 5'7" and had a black cape on. He had almond shaped black eyes and ridge over his brow much like an iguana or a Neanderthal might have…. He's always very stern…. I can sense that he's a male. He tells the others what to

do. The smaller ones are probably about 4 to 4.5 feet. They were working for him, I believe.

After struggling for a few moments she found that she was able to move. She reached out to her right side and grabbed a small gray figure with a round head and huge glistening eyes by the throat. The cloaked being's throat felt like a roll of quarters. Audrey recalled, "There was talking in my head, 'Watch out for the mother.' It seemed to be coming from the one at the end of the bed. They then proceeded to try to get control of me. I had sat up and moved to the side of my bed and get my footing. I headed for the bedroom door and opened it. There were smaller beings outside in my hallway by the door. Then I felt a burning sensation and that's all I remember."

Audrey says she regained consciousness and found herself hovering in the center of her room. Swiftly, she passed through the mirror on a dresser at the foot of her bed, feet first. All of a sudden she could see the night sky, amber lights, and a single blue light that flickered above her. She looked down and saw her house fading into the distance.

Once she had arrived on the craft she was placed into a cocoon-like encasement in a gel-like substance that she could breathe. She felt warm and at first didn't realize that she was floating in a viscous, pale, greenish-gray fluid. She was able to look around the room and saw five other humans who appeared to be unconscious in the same kind of gel suspended in the air in glass-like cylinders or boxes.

The room was round and there were three doorways leading in different directions. The Greys were busy guiding gurneys with people on them down the hallway and returning for more. When they realized Audrey was awake they did something that made her lose consciousness.

She awoke naked on a metal table in a huge, round room, surrounded by beings of many different races. She had never seen some of them before. There were two or three 6-foot-tall humanoid types dressed in white and blue with blond hair and blue eyes. They seemed to be glowing. The tall being with the ridge over its brow was standing in the background, just observing or supervising. Several shorter Greys and two or three tall blue creatures with human features faced the table in the arena in which Audrey was the subject being studied.

A fight-or-flight response kicked in, and she attempted to escape but fell from the table. Her next memory was of hovering 8 to 12 inches above the floor.

There was a tiny being, about 2 feet tall at eye level, directly in front of her with a very thin, wormlike body. It had two long legs, two long arms, and a parasitic-type mouth. When she reached out and grabbed him, he emitted a horrifying sound similar to a fox's scream. Audrey stated, "I really felt bad after I did it. It was hurt and it was lying on the ground. I picked it up and it shook itself off and it ran. The beings were watching this and seemed pleased that I did this. They levitated me back up toward the table. Then a big machine came down and attached to the back of my spine where it meets the neck. The machine attached to my spine and I felt a burning sensation—not any pain really, but a burning." The next morning she noticed marks on her spine and photographed them.

Audrey asked why they had put the machine on her neck. They said that they were altering or activating her DNA and doing something pertaining somehow to enlightenment.

Next she was rolled onto her back and a claw-like device removed her right eye and placed something behind the socket. Audrey stated, "This took my eye out. There was a long sharp needle like device that put something in. I didn't feel pain, but I felt fear. For days after my eye watered like crazy and it still does."

She was then led to a classroom with rows of desks facing a chalkboard. All the desks were full. A human-looking teacher walked up to Audrey and told her that everything the group needs to know is lying dormant in them and will activate when she and the others need it. After that she had several classroom experiences. She asked, "What's the point of learning when we don't remember anything?" and was told, "We have everything we need to know and when the time comes it will activate. It's inside you and you'll be aware of everything you need to be aware of when the time comes. It's so irritating because I do remember some symbols. I've written them down." Today, from time to time, she feels a rush of energy and suddenly has flashes of memories of all this information.

Audrey doesn't remember being returned to her bedroom, just waking up in her bed. As she went about her daily activities, she became

Audrey's photograph of the black helicopter above her home. Credit: Audrey Hewins.

cognizant of the fact that a black helicopter was hovering outside her window. She said that it remained close to her house for the entire day, so she took her camera outside and photographed it. She added, "They'd been following me around before, but this time it was different. The night before a woman who claimed to be an extraterrestrial called me. Then all of a sudden there was a horrible screeching sound that hurt my ears. It bothered my ears for some time. It was almost like the military knew they were coming before I did."

At this point in my interview with Audrey, all of her abduction accounts had initiated in her bedroom at night and, aside from the bruising and photo, might be interpreted as sleep-related hallucinations or dreams. It was important to know if she had ever been taken from an external environment, such as while driving, hiking, fishing, etc. She confirmed that she had been on more than one occasion. One time, she was to meet her sister at a prearranged time and was passing a race track near her home anticipating her turn in the road. As if only a moment had passed, she found herself on a different unfamiliar road. Her engine wasn't running and she was seated idly in the driver's seat. She had lost 45 minutes without an acceptable, prosaic explanation for the missing time. Missing time is a marker of alien abduction mentioned in the majority of lifelong and one-occurrence abduction events. Her second missing-time event occurred on a highway near her home and was similar to the first.

Our next case of alien abduction is different, because the witness's first experience seems to have occurred when he was driving in a remote area. It is not as detailed, but due to the witness's reputation as a credible public figure, it should be told.

"Andrew Stevens" is a veteran science journalist formerly from Colorado Springs, Colorado. Nearly 10 years ago, he experienced missing time while driving from his home to his parent's residence in Montrose, Colorado. Two days earlier, he had taken a bus to Cheyenne, Wyoming, to purchase a 1990 White Chevy Cargo Van that he had found online. He'd stayed overnight at a motel in Cheyenne with the intention of returning to his home in Colorado Springs for a nap before he departed for Montrose. He fell into a deep slumber and awoke later than he anticipated, filled with a sense of urgency to arrive at his parent's home by 4 a.m. His parents had appointed him executor of their estate, and he had an appointment to attend an important family legal meeting on Monday morning.

The route along US 50, southwest of Colorado Springs, can be treacherous in the autumn during a freak snowstorm over the 11,312 foot-high Monarch Pass in the Sawatch Mountains, with its hairpin-turn switchbacks and strong winds. But the meeting was extremely important and he had to chance encountering inclement weather. He had not planned his weekend well.

Andrew had departed on his 4 hour 45 minute trip at 11:15 p.m. and expected to arrive by 4:15 or 4:30 a.m. at the latest, allowing for two stops along the way. After leaving Colorado Springs, he traveled along CO 115 South to Canon City where he stopped at an all night gas station. He checked the odometer and calculated his gas mileage. It was 12:15 a.m. and he was on schedule. From there he headed west 57 miles to Salida and west toward Monarch Pass. The next sizable town would be Gunnison, 65 miles west of Salida and on the other side of Monarch Pass. He anticipated that he'd arrive in Gunnison by 3 a.m.

Luck was with him. It was a beautiful, bright night with excellent driving conditions. Manning the wheel of his new van, Andrew began his ascent toward the top of Monarch Pass and the Continental Divide. The near-full moon lit up the mountainous terrain illuminating a breathtaking view of the surrounding mountains. Looking off to his left, he took in a stunning vista of the craggy snow-capped mountain ridges in the distance. He noticed a peach-colored light in the sky that seemed to be approaching very rapidly and was drawn to its unusual color and flight pattern. Soon he began to wonder if he was having his first UFO sighting. His next memory was of stopping for several deer that were blocking the highway. There were lights in the forest and he saw what appeared to be a humanoid figure. Then the lights were directly over his van. Nothing more.

Suddenly and without warning, he found himself back near Salida. It was 4:05 a.m. and he was nearly 20 miles east of where he had been in what seemed like a moment before. He said that the experience reminded him of the way it feels to undergo surgery: you are awake, you receive anesthesia, and suddenly you're awake again. Feeling bewildered and shaken, he sat for a moment attempting to rationalize how he could have turned around without realizing it. He was certain that he hadn't stopped, except for the deer in the road. He continued back up Monarch Pass to Gunnison and on toward Montrose, arriving at 7:10 a.m. His odometer did not register the additional 20 miles. It had taken 8 hours to travel 166 miles.

Andrew told only a few close friends about his missing-time event and attempted to stash it in the recesses of his mind. But it came to the surface over and over again through the years, especially when an unidentifiable craft descended toward him. He periodically awoke with haunting, dreamlike memories of what seemed like ET visitation. This had never happened prior to the incident on Monarch Pass. He married and his wife was sometimes awoken by his apparent sleep-talking in a language she had never heard before. He was looking for answers, but didn't know where to turn to. His professional position placed him in the public eye. It would be risky to report it to a UFO investigative group. If it leaked out, it would mean professional suicide.

Finally, he found a licensed therapist that was trained in the use of hypnosis and underwent a series of hypnotic regressions. His memory remained vague, but fleeting images of information emerged. Under hypnosis it was revealed that the deer were a "screen memory" for a group of ETs that stopped Andrew's van in the road. Screen memories are a way that ETs manipulate the human mind into perceiving a frightening image as non-threatening and are common during the procurement process. Individuals observe what they think is deer, elk, large owls, etc. immediately before their missing-time event, but hypnosis later reveals that they are in reality non-human entities.

In Andrew's case, the deer approached his car and removed him from it. He recalled finding himself in an alien environment with three Grey beings—two young ones and an older teacher—who didn't seem to understand his behavior. All were observing an image of a dark planet surrounded by a vast red-orange energy field. Space was warped and a pulsing, luminous electromagnetic field was visible. Next he saw a very large moon coming out of the night sky. He was not able to recall additional details that would enlighten us on this information.

Andrew holds an important professional position and cannot reveal his identity to the public due to the possible negative consequences. His case is interesting, but is largely circumstantial and based only upon a single witness anecdotal report. The next account of alien abduction is far more complex. It spans nearly 60 years and is supported by the statements of witnesses deemed credible by MUFON investigators. I have interviewed Thomas Reed several times over the phone and through e-mail exchanges, and he has submitted evidence to me with regard to his mother's statements, his father's professional and political positions, his polygraph exam, and his brother's physical evidence case.

The Howard and Nancy Reed family's multigenerational abduction case is significant in the annals of UFO abduction history. Thomas and his younger brother Matthew spent their early childhood years on an 80-acre quarter horse farm in a rural area of Sheffield, Massachusetts, with his mother and grandmother. They had moved to the Berkshires in 1962, Thomas said, following his parent's divorce, when he was 2 years old. His mother Nancy owned and operated The Village on the Green Restaurant until she married her second husband, Howard Reed. He adopted her two sons and their names were changed from MacIntyre to Reed.[3]

In 1954, 15-year-old Nancy, her mother, brother Bob, and Bob's 16-year-old girlfriend were spending the night at a rented cottage on Moosehead Lake in the sparsely inhabited northwestern quadrant of the state. Nancy awoke in the middle of the night and felt the presence of several beings in her room that seemed to be observing her. An arcing light penetrated through the window and gave her a glimpse of the unearthly presence she sensed was in her room: short, pudgy figures. She attempted to speak but discovered that she was paralyzed and unable to move under her own control. She grasped the comforter and attempted to move her body off the bed, but to no avail. She felt as if her body was being manipulated—her lower extremities twisted back and forth—but she could not feel the pressure of touch. She described it as the sensation one would experience if confined to the inside of a manikin. Her experience persisted for what seemed like a very long time, but she finally regained control of her body at daybreak. She felt nauseated and sat on the corner of her bed before making her way to the kitchen where her mother found her. Thomas said that her brother's girlfriend, who'd been sleeping in a room on the other side of the cottage, had a similar experience that night. This was her only memory of an unearthly presence until Thomas and Matthew were young boys on the family farm in Sheffield.

In September of 1966, Nancy's young sons observed orbs in their bedroom. One was near the upper right side of the room and about the size of a small dinner plate. It remained in position for some time before it drifted toward the left wall. Thomas described it as resembling a cylindrical ring with a transparent, rolling, whitewashed-looking center (like a cloud), with a crisp, thin, bright, bluish outer ring. There were others that were less noticeable, but still visible to Thomas. Afraid to move, he sensed that it was alive and watching him as he was attempting to discern a face or eyes. Thomas thought that he was observing ghosts, but changed his mind when, days later, he and his brother had what can only be described as an alien intrusion.

The boys recalled that they were standing at the top of their staircase with several 4.5- to 5-foot-tall ghostly looking figures. In what seemed like seconds, the ground changed under their feet and they found themselves at the top of the tree line on the edge of their property, where they were met by additional entities. The boys were taken into a tarnished, dull-looking craft that had the external appearance of a giant turtle shell resting on the ground. They encountered beings that were somewhat like the small, thin, stereotypical Grey, but different. Their physical appearance was more human, as if they were half human and half Grey, with large eyes that might have been covered by a lens, but not as large as today's stereotypical Grey.

Thomas observed an image of what appeared to be eight to 10 groups of galaxy clusters in the shape of a boot on a large screen on the wall. There was also a willow tree image that seemed so symbolic to him that he later drew it. The beings communicated to Thomas that he was serving an important purpose for them as a participant in a biological study. He believes that it pertains to gene splicing for their own benefit with a focus upon the human immune system and genetics. When they had served their purpose, the boys were released and awoke to find themselves in their bedroom.

Thomas and Matthew were curious to find the location that they had been taken to, so defying his mother's orders, Thomas rode his horse to the site. He wrote of it, "Although I do not recall a lot from that night, it really hit me in the stomach when I took my horse to the top right corner of that field, passing a huge boulder, and coming across a wishbone tree. I had to lower my head under the branches and there was the spot...I had never been there before (willingly), but knew the path."

Nancy awoke one late summer night in 1967 to discover that her 5- and 7-year-old sons were missing. Turning on the floodlights for a better view of the yard, she stepped outside to begin her search of the driveways and trails on her extensive property. Unable to find them at first, she headed for the Appalachian Trail on the back side of the farm for an unencumbered view of the land below. From the trail, she was able to see that her sons were in her driveway and made her way to the two youngsters, whose behavior she said was unusual. They were simply "not themselves."

Her sons recalled watching darkness fall upon their bedroom, as flashes of light played upon their bedroom window. At first they thought that it was lightning and anticipated thunderclaps, but none came. Thomas told Matthew to look at a ball of light about 20 feet outside their second-story bedroom window. Suddenly a white light exploded and engulfed the room. Abruptly, an attic hatch began to rattle and the boys became frightened. Matthew wanted Thomas to open the heavy bedroom door and make an escape down the hall to the safety of his mother's bedroom. Thomas recalls only that he felt like he'd fallen forward in a tuck and roll position, as if gravity was being manipulated. He felt the momentary sensation of weightlessness and what seemed like a whiteout. When Thomas didn't reply to Matthew's request, he looked down and found that his older brother was no longer on the lower bunk. Terrified now, Matthew struggled to open the latch that would release him to the hallway that led to his mother's bedroom. Finally, he was free and running to the safety of her bed—hiding behind her resting body that did not stir. His grandmother lay still in another bed in the room.

As he lay trembling with fear, four apparitions entered the bedroom and glided toward the bed, followed by a smaller, clearly defined figure that was walking. Despite his attempts to wake his mother, she remained in a deep sleep, as if she were in a coma. Two figures floated upon his mother's side of the bed, while two remained by the doorway. The fifth figure seemed to raise its long insect-like legs and stepped upon his grandmother's bed, but she did not stir. Nancy would not wake until after they left the room, despite Matthew's attempts to rouse her. The fifth figure backed out of the room all the while staring at Matthew.

Nancy finally awoke, and Matthew informed her that Thomas was missing. She searched for him and then after hearing a loud bang, similar to a heavy door slamming, everything went blank. Thomas found himself on a craft much like the one he had been on the year before. He was feeling nervous and yelled for his younger brother, whose presence Thomas found comforting, and Matthew was brought to him. His next recall was of being returned to his yard. Thomas found himself on a hill off the driveway and Matthew was standing in the driveway. Both boys were bewildered and disoriented. They had almost no memory of where they had been or how they arrived at this location, but they did recall some of their experience. Nancy hastened from her vantage point on the Appalachian Trail to her sons whose eyes were locked upon one another. She took her pale, frightened sons to the kitchen for juice, children's aspirin, and wet towels. The boys finally fell asleep on the living room sofa, as their mother watched over them. Later, Thomas looked for the location where the craft had landed. He found evidence that it was not far from the 1966 landing area.

The last of the Reed family's Massachusetts encounters occurred in October 1969, following an equestrian event in a nearby resort town. The family was headed home in their station wagon, with Nancy at the wheel at dusk. Thomas remembers that his grandmother became fixated on lights out the left rear side of their vehicle, and then he and his brother observed what looked like searchlights and then a flying strip mall behind trees that lined the road. Realizing the magnitude of what was about to occur and the memories of prior events brought terror to Nancy. She accelerated, but moments later, the engine died. He heard what sounded like stones hitting the underside of the station wagon, then silence, followed by an eruption of crickets and katydids chirping.

Moments later, the family found themselves in separate holding areas in a hot, humid, stale alien environment. A gruff figure grabbed 9-year-old Thomas's left arm and quickly escorted him down a hallway and into an examining room with crisp, cool air. He saw two horrific figures focusing upon the wall, two more at the foot of a table, and one in the rear right-hand corner. He was forced to lie on a silver-white table, but terror overtook him and he sprung from the table and darted out of the room. He entered an angled open area, as wide as a basketball court, with a single hall off it to the left and multiple halls to the right, and heard voices. But moments later he was captured and returned to his room.

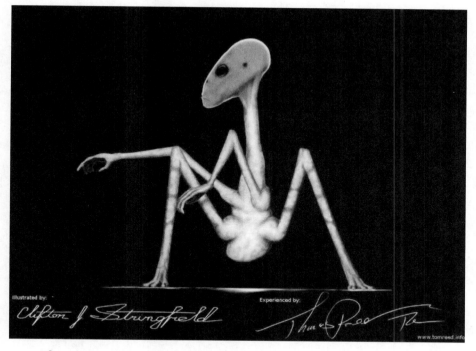

Thomas Reed's insectoid being observed in 1969. Credit: Sketched by Clifton Stringfield from Thomas Reed's original 1969 drawing. Rights are owned by Thomas Reed.

Back on the table in the examining room, Thomas's movement was restricted by an oval-shaped apparatus, similar to the lid on a tanning bed that lowered from the ceiling and clamped over his torso. He sensed tapping on the back of his head and recalled that stones that resembled shiny raisins were placed on his face, chest, and leg. When his exam was completed he was returned to the huge, open holding area, but did not see his family.

They were returned to the car...separately. Strangely, it was now facing in the opposite direction from what it had been. (This has been reported to me several times.) Thomas was seated behind the driver's seat, his mother in the passenger seat, and his brother was curled up on the back seat in a fetal position. Through the car window, Thomas saw his grandmother walking aimlessly in the middle of the road.

He walked toward her as she turned toward a store. She walked to a stroller and grasped the handle, guiding it back and forth as if she were attempting to calm a baby. Thomas led his grandmother, who seemed to be in a state of shock, out of the store. Halfway back to the car, Thomas said, she stopped walking and her body began to shake, as if she were attempting to catch her breath. His devastated grandmother broke down sobbing and repeating "Oh my God!" over and over again. She yelled for Nancy as Thomas guided her back to the car. His mother was now awake and drove home without uttering a single word.

Thomas said that this encounter was the last straw for Nancy. She sold the Massachusetts property and moved her sons to the Litchfield/Canaan area, and then West Haven, Connecticut. She had already met Howard Reed, whom she later married.

The elusive physical evidence that would prove scientifically that the Reed family has experienced an alien abduction came in the spring of 2009, when Matthew had a strange experience while driving in his SUV. It was a beautiful evening, so after dropping off his friend at about 10:15, he decided to take the long route home. He remembered stopping at a traffic light and turning to wave goodbye to his friend. In the blink of an eye and without prosaic explanation, he realized that he was no longer at the traffic light, but near a corn field. His shoes were caked in mud, but he had no memory of walking in wet soil, and his clock indicated that it was an hour later than it had been a moment before. He returned home and made a formal report to the Mutual UFO Network. MUFON's rapid response Star Team found physical evidence on the car including extreme radiation readings (not in the surrounding area) and magnetic effects. Holding a compass in his hand, the MUFON field investigator walked slowly along the driver's side starting at the hood and moving toward the trunk. He held the compass 6 to 8 inches from the metallic surface. As he approached the rear of the vehicle, the compass needle began to rotate in a counterclockwise direction. He turned and walked in the opposite direction and the needle stopped, then swept in a clockwise direction. An experiment with his own vehicle produced none of the effects that he'd just observed on Matthew's SUV. (Note: A compass needle whirled when it was placed over the trunk of Betty Hill's car in 1961.)

Thomas believes that his abduction experiences have been ongoing into his adult life and have also affected his children. One night, he awoke to find his shoulders and head on his pillow, but his lower body and legs were stretched up near the ceiling fan. He couldn't breathe. He couldn't swallow and felt like his throat was clogged. Then he was partway over the tanning bed. His entire body was elevated diagonally between his bed and his tanning bed. His feet were over the tanning bed and he was moving toward the second story window. It felt as if there was no gravity and he was in flight. It was 2:33 a.m. At that point, the room darkened, and he found himself back in his bed breathing normally. He shot up out of bed and ran into the master bath and ran water on his face and head. He then heard a scream from his son's bedroom. His son also had memories of a light in his bedroom and what looked like a silver silk pillowcase over his bed. Both suspected that they had been taken.

Thomas' case has been investigated by Tennessee MUFON Star Team investigator Steve White, who asked him to submit to a polygraph exam. They used a licensed polygraph service, owned and operated by a retired police officer in Knoxville, Tennessee. In two questions, after the officer and he had discussed the events and history in detail for over three hours, Thomas was asked if he had intentionally lied about his 1966 experiences concerning the craft and if he had intentionally lied about his experiences on the craft. Thomas passed the exam with no evidence of deception.

This multigenerational abduction case has many of the earmarks of a true series of events. It is highly complicated and has multiple witnesses. I have interviewed Thomas Reed and examined his and MUFON's files on his case. As in all abduction claims, evidence collection is ongoing and will eventually lead to a final determination on this case.

As we approach the end of this book, there is one more issue that begs discussion. It is an important issue to many of the people that have contacted us. They wonder if individuals are really being abducted by alien entities or if there is another reasonable explanation? In our search for the truth, it has been necessary for us to examine several alternative hypotheses, including psychological states (already discussed throughout this book), demonic possession, and astral entity attachment.

The alien abduction experience is interpreted by certain groups as something other than UFO-related. Many people fear that nocturnal visitation is a sign of entity attachment, not extraterrestrial visitation, especially when paranormal activity accompanies the experience. Denise and I discovered that 88 percent of the experiencers in the Marden-Stoner study had observed paranormal (psi) activity in their homes after an abduction experience. The majority reported light orbs that sometimes expanded into Grey entities and poltergeist activity. There is frequently electromagnetic interference, such as lights bulbs and appliances blowing out or electronic equipment functioning on its own, even when unplugged. Watches, cameras, computers, and scanners malfunction for no prosaic reason. Additionally, experiencers report that windows and doors open and close on their own. Our study suggests that this activity is sometimes similar to but probably unrelated to the phenomena pertaining to a ghost or disembodied spirit presence as reported by the non-abduction experiencer group, such as temperature changes, mist clouds, strange sounds, strange odors, and cold spots.

During our exploration of poltergeist activity in association with negative entities, we discovered that a tiny percentage of experiencers endured horrific abuse as children, and psychologically separated from their physical bodies through a process of dissociation. This separation of self became a coping mechanism that ensured the child's psychological survival. But later in life, these victims of abuse remain prone to a dissociative process. In its mild form, it manifests as being mildly detached from one's surroundings, such as in daydreaming. In its acute form, it can manifest as multiple personality disorder (dissociative identity disorder). In a period of extreme stress among those with its acute form, the individual might experience a dissociative fugue state, which is similar to "blacking out" due to the consumption of excessive amounts of alcohol. One's identity might be temporarily forgotten and a period of lost time can occur. This, however, is extremely rare. Academic studies conducted by Kenneth Ring and Christopher J. Rosing, (the 1990 Omega 2 Project) and Robert B. LeLieuvre, Lester Valez, and Michael Freeman (the 2010 Omega

3 Project) indicate that there is a slightly elevated rate of dissociation among some self-identified abduction experiencers. An alternative explanation for the development of a dissociative coping process might be found in the abduction itself.

An alternative hypothesis is the belief that a segment of the abduction experiencer population is being influenced by astral entities rather than extraterrestrial beings during out-of-body experiences, dreaming or lucid dreaming, or astral projection experiences. Paul Hamden, a medium, has addressed this issue. Mediumship has a reputation as being a product of the human imagination, but Paul's messages from three groups of alleged ETs (Zetas, Pleiadian, and Anunnaki), have attracted the attention of a Canadian scientist who is studying the validity of the information given through Paul. The scientist has stated, in a series of technical papers, that Paul has channeled scientifically verifiable information far beyond his educational level and the scope of his knowledge.

Paul states that most races are here to support us and that we are very important to the cosmological structure of the universal consciousness, but that some beings do not have the best intentions for our race. The ET groups have stated through Paul that beings from the astral realm live in the evolving energetic environment and that it is separate from the physical (although closely aligned) and spirit realms. These are non-physical entities but are experienced as real by the human mind.[4]

The astral realms are said to be a chaotic compilation of the collective human mind (the developing collective consciousness), and are part of the ascension process of human consciousness. All thoughts are part of this grid of consciousness and all thoughts hold some level of frequency. Some thoughts and entities resonate at a higher level toward an elevated state of being and consciousness, whereas other entities are seeking to own the energies of humanity. This lower state of being is in conflict with the higher state of being and wishes to be in control of the human collective consciousness. Paul says, "It is seen that the collective human consciousness will evolve past this current process and ultimately will be the mechanism for humans to be able to communicate telepathically with each other."[5]

The ETs inform us that astral entities, beings called the "collectors" or "controllers" by some, are attracted to humanity's behavior. Some entities who are from other interdimensional states, reside in the astral realm and are entering into human thought processes during enforced encounters, as generated by different behaviors of humans. They state that many of the negative experiences reported by abduction experiencers have been perpetrated by astral entities, not extraterrestrials. It is important for us to know that there have been far fewer humans abducted than is commonly believed, and that screen memory technology is often used as a technique of disguising the true identity of the entities.

Paul informed me, in a private communication, that aside from the encounter process as mentioned above, substance misuse and other negative human behaviors open the channel for astral entities to attach to the human thought processes and that these entities can be cleared away by meditation, and the modification of a human's behaviors toward a higher level of consciousness and understanding of one's own existence.

Astral entities, he said, have an agenda to control and feed off human emotions. Some believe these entities masquerade as extraterrestrial beings and mislead people by informing them that they are special, have varied and different abilities (none which are ever actually manifested), while at the same time they inflict emotional and psychological harm upon their victims. He believes that in *some* cases people, who believe they have been abducted or accosted, are actually under the influence of astral entities.

The ETs have channeled to Paul information that although they are different than Earthlings in many ways, they possess a collective consciousness that guides their behavior in relation to one another. Yet, they have free will, and will never harm one of their own or another being.

They are puzzled by some of the more primitive aspects of man's behavior, such as greed and the horrors of violence. They have expressed concern that humanity's consciousness must move ahead on an evolutionary scale for its own survival. They can guide, but they rarely intercede. They are only an advanced species—not the hand of God.

Astral entity attachment sounds similar (although somewhat different) to demonic possession, as interpreted by the Christian Information Ministries and other Fundamentalist Christian ideologies. They believe that Satan and his fallen angels are involved in UFO sightings and alien abduction and use their power to entrap the spiritually naïve in order to deceive them by leading them away from their faith in Jesus Christ. Faith is placed in the chance of salvation by an advanced extraterrestrial species that is leading the ascension process for the chosen few, when in reality it is a grand deception that will lead to an explosion of demonic activity during the last days before Christ returns.[6] (Paul doesn't talk about ascension for a chosen few. It is only an evolutionary step in human consciousness development.)

The Roman Catholic Church has offered an opinion on extraterrestrial encounters that differs from the Fundamentalist Christian point of view. The late Monsignor Corrado Balducci, a demonologist and priest close to Pope John Paul II, looking into extraterrestrial encounters, spoke out about ET contact. He emphasized that ET contact is not demonic or related to entity attachment, explaining that we must view extraterrestrials as part of God's creation—not angels or devils.

His opinion is based upon the fact that many UFO eyewitnesses are highly educated, qualified observers who did not previously believe in the reality of ET visitation. Additionally, thousands of people from around the world have observed UFOs and their non-human crews. Although some of these sightings have prosaic explanations, many do not. He advised Christians that the craft are technologically structured and the ETs aboard them are humanoid beings of a physical and spiritual nature, probably more highly spiritual than humans.

To those who deny it's reality, the Monsignor wrote, "Let me add one more important point: The general a priori-scepticism, the systematic, total denial, damages, even destroys the basic value of the human testimony with grave and incalculable consequences, since it is indeed the fundament of human society, if individual, social or religious. Of course there is always one or the other exemption, there are errors and lies, but generally all our life is based on what we learned from others. It is unthinkable to live without this basic confidence, unimaginable are the consequences of a general negation of the human experience on the individual, social and religious life. It would destroy the very fundament of any human society!"[7]

Father Jose Funes, Director the Vatican Observatory, named to his position by Pope Benedict XVI, stated in 2008 that extraterrestrial beings should be considered a part of God's creation. Just as God created life on earth, he said, he may have created multiple forms of life throughout the universe that might be similar to humans, but different in many ways. "This is not in contrast with the faith, because we cannot place limits on the creative freedom of God...To use St. Francis' words, if we consider earthly creatures as 'brothers' and 'sisters', why can't we also speak of an 'extraterrestrial brother?'" he said.[8]

As we move toward the end of this book, we consider it imperative to state that Denise and I have carefully weighed each of the above hypotheses and believe that each might pertain to a particular type of experience. However, one alone should not be considered an all encompassing explanation for alien abduction.

We have spoken with individuals who have been hospitalized for psychiatric disorders that appear to be unrelated to the alien abduction phenomenon, although they initially feared that they were experiencing abduction. Yet, it is important to state that numerous psychological studies have demonstrated that those who meet the criteria for having experienced an alien abduction have no more psychiatric illness and are no more fantasy-prone than the general population. Others appear to have suffered a spiritual crisis or entity attachment, and have sought the assistance of psychic healers or church representatives. Sometimes, entity attachments have been removed and religious intervention and/or exorcism has been accomplished. But many, many others during the past 65 years have observed structured craft that can out-fly and out-maneuver anything on earth.

The majority of experiencers have conscious, continuous recall of at least one close encounter with these crafts and the observation of non-human entities prior to an abduction while they were outside their homes. Many were not alone and have witnesses that remember the event. They are aware of having been examined on a craft in an alien environment by what can best be described as scientists from another solar system. They carry psychological scars, such as fear, anxiety, and trauma from being taken against their will, and physical scars from the excision of circular tissue extraction, patterned puncture wounds, migraine headaches, sensitivity to light, and CFIDS. All of this supports the extraterrestrial hypothesis of alien visitation and the abduction of humans. It seems to us that we should be looking at the evidence and giving credence to those whose experiences cannot be adequately explained as psychologically generated or related to entity attachment, whether demonic or astral. Only then can real healing occur and greater understanding ensue.

Notes

Introduction

1. Friedman and Marden, *Captured! The Betty And Barney Hill Experience*, p. 183

2. The term "abduction experiencer" is used throughout this book as a neutral term meaning that the individual believes that he or she has been abducted by aliens. It does not imply that the person has had a real experience. It might be real or it might be imaginary.

Chapter 2

1. Project Blue Book Special Report #14.

2. Stanton T. Friedman, "UFOs," *Science Was Wrong*.

3. Saunders and Harkins, 1968, Appendix A, *Ufos? Yes!: Where the Condon Committee Went Wrong*

4. Ibid. p. 131.

5. Edward Condon, "Conclusions and Recommendations," *The Scientific Study Of Unidentified Flying Objects.* p. 28.

6. National Academy of Sciences, "Review of the University of Colorado Report on Unidentified Flying Objects."

7. Lee Speigel, "Charles Halt, Former Air Force Colonel, Accuses U.S. Of UFO Cover-Up," Huffington Post (September

24, 2012). *www.huffingtonpost.com/2012/09/24/ufo-secrets-turn-out-to-be-strong-opinions_n_1907492.html*

8. Ibid.

9. Lord Martin Rees, the U.K. Astronomer Royal's statement on September 19, 2012.

10. Nick Pope's statement at the National Atomic Testing Museum in Las Vegas, during a panel discussion on UFOs. September 22, 2012.

11. Colonel Bill Coleman's statement at the National Atomic Testing Museum in Las Vegas, during a panel discussion on UFOs. September 22, 2012

Chapter 4

1. *www.heavens-above.com* and *www.wunderground.com*.

2. I am certified by the National Guild of Hypnotists. My knowledge comes from advanced training in hypnotic regression.

3. Hypnotic Regression Manual, "Interesting Facts About Forensic Hypnosis," p. 12.

Chapter 5

4. As noted in Ed Stoner's dive log.

5. Checked on Mapquest at *www.mapquest.com*.

Chapter 6

1. This information was supplied to me by Denise in a written document dated 6/8/2012.

Chapter 7

1. Dozens of experiencers have described an identical room.

2. It is commonplace for hypnotized individuals to remember more after the session has ended, about their experience after the initial memory emerges. This also true of recall without hypnosis.

3. This scene has been described by David Jacobs (*The Threat*) and Barbara Lamb ("Are Human ET Hybrids in Our Future?").

Chapter 8

1. This was a theme of the "Experiencers Speak" conference held near Portland, Maine, in September 2012.
2. John F. Kilstrom, "Hypnosis and Memory," *http://ist-socrates.berkeley.edu/~kihlstrm/hypnosis_l&m2003.htm*
3. "The Marden-Stoner Study on Commonalities Among Abduction Experiencers" can be read at *www.kathleen-marden.com.*

Chapter 9

1. This chapter is based upon a written account by "Jennie Henderson" of her experiences. Jennie is a real person whose identity is anonymous.

Chapter 10

1. Jennie was diagnosed months later with chronic fatigue and immune dysfunction syndrome; 38 percent of the participants in the "Marden-Stoner Study on Commonalities Among Abduction Experiencers" have a formal diagnosis, although it is prevalent in less than 1 percent of the general population.
2. This is a segment of MUFON's mission statement. The full statement is posted at *www.mufon.com.*
3. "Hypnagogic Hallucinations." *www.patient.co.uk/doctor/hypnagogic-hallucinations.htm.*

Chapter 11

1. These symptoms have been reported by many abduction researchers, including Budd Hopkins, Yvonne Smith, Leo Sprinkle, and John Carpenter.

2. These are commonalities that were discovered by several different abduction investigators, such as Budd Hopkins, Derrel Sims, and Leonard Stringfield, and were confirmed on the "Marden-Stoner Study on Commonalities Among Abduction Experiencers."

3. "Ethics Code for Abduction Investigation and Treatment," MUFON Field Investigator's Manual.

4. This is required by MUFON.

Chapter 12

1. For additional information, see John G. Fuller's *Incident at Exeter.*

Chapter 13

1. This scene has been described by David Jacobs (*The Threat*), and Barbara Lamb ("Are Human-ET Hybrids in Our Future?"). Jennie's experience was documented prior to the first report in any book or article.

2. Jennie documented this in the 1970s, prior to any publication on this phenomenon.

Chapter 14

1. Stan Romanek, *Messages*. Laboratory analysis of the stain on the back of the woman's nightgown that Stan woke up in revealed that it was a chemical substance with anomalous properties.

Chapter 15

1. Several groups have been reported, including Greys; insectoids; Reptilians; blue, gold, and white entities; brown entities; and human types, such as blond Nordics and 8-foot-tall Annunaki.

Chapter 16

1. All quotes in this chapter regarding D. Lynn Bishop are taken from her unpublished manuscript.

2. This information is taken directly from my September 2012 interview with Audrey Hewins.

3. Information from the Reed family case is derived from several sources and has been approved by Thomas Reed in this accurate version of his family's story. These include my 11-5-2012 interview with Thomas Reed, Mike Gibson's article "The Reed Family's Alien Nightmare" (*www.metropulse.com/news/2012/feb/15/reed-familys-alien-nightmare*), the Reed family's interview with Lorin Cutts, and Steve White's article "Thomas E. Reed Family Abduction."

4. William Treuniet and Paul Hamden, July 2012.

5. Quoted from a private communication with Paul Hamden.

6. The Christian Information Ministries, "UFOs And Alien Abductions," 6/11/2003.

7. Monsignor Corrado Balducci, "UFOs and Extraterrestrials: A Problem for the Church?"

8. John Thavis, Catholic News Service article.

Bibliography

Balducci, Monsignor Corrado. *http://rense.com/general12/filers8101.htm* (visited 3/7/2013).

———. "UFOs and Extraterrestrials: A Problem for the Church?" *www.pufoin.com/pufoin_perspective/et_church.php.* (visited 12/11/2012).

Blackmore, Susan. "Abduction by Aliens or Sleep Paralysis?" *Skeptical Inquirer Magazine.* (May/June 1998) *www.ufoevidence.org/documents/doc817.htm* (visited 7/2/2009).

Bullard, Thomas E. "Comparative Analysis of UFO Abduction Reports." 1987.

———. "What's New in Alien Abduction? Has the Story Changed in 30 Years?" *MUFON 1999 International UFO Symposium Proceedings.* p. 170–199.

Bloecher, Ted, Aphrodite Clamar, and Budd Hopkins. "Final Report on the Psychological Testing of UFO 'Abductees.'" Mt. Rainier, Maryland: Fund for UFO Research, 1985.

Cahill, Kelly. "Are Multiple Witnesses and Scientific Anomalies Enough Proof of UFO Reality?" *MUFON 1999 International UFO Symposium Proceedings.* p. 160–169.

Carpenter, John. "The Significance of Multiple Witness Abductions." *MUFON 1996 International UFO Symposium Proceedings.* p. 119–137.

———. The Reality of the Abduction Phenomenon." *MUFON 1991 International Symposium Proceedings*. Mutual UFO Network, 1991.

Condon, Edward U. *Scientific Study of Unidentified Flying* Objects. New York: Bantam Press, 1969.

Friedman, Stanton and Kathleen Marden. *Captured! The Betty and Barney Hill UFO Experience*. Franklin Lakes, New Jersey: New Page Books, 2007.

Friedman, Stanton T. *Flying Saucers and Science*. Franklin Lakes, New Jersey: New Page Books, 2008.

Friedman, Stanton and Kathleen Marden. *Science Was Wrong*. Franklin Lakes, New Jersey: New Page Books, 2010.

Fuller, John G. *The Incident at Exeter*. New York: G.P. Puttnam's Sons, 1966.

———. "The Flying Saucer Fiasco" *Look Magazine* (May 14, 1968).

Gibson, Mike. "The Reed Family's Alien Nightmare." *www.metropulse.com/news/2012/feb/15/reed-familys-alien-nightmare* (visited 10/14/2012).

Heavens Above. *www.heavens-above.com* (visited 6/24/2012).

Hopkins, Budd. *Intruders*. New York: Random House, 1987.

———. *Witnessed*. New York: Pocket Books, 1996.

Hopkins, Budd and Carol Rainey. *Sight Unseen*. New York: Atria, 2003.

Howe, Linda Moulton. *Glimpses of Other Realities*. New Orleans: Paper Chase Press, 1998.

Hufford, David J. *The Terror that Comes in the Night*. Philadelphia: University of Pennsylvania Press, 1982.

"Hypnagogic Hallucinations." *www.patient.co.uk/doctor/Hypnagogic-Hallucinations.htm* . (visited 12/3/2012)

Hypnotic Regression. Mottin and Johnson Institute of Hypnosis. New Florence, Missouri, 2012.

Jacobs, David. *www.ufoabduction.com*. (visited 12/23/2011).

———. *Secret Life*. New York: Simon & Schuster, 1992.

———. *The Threat*. New York: Simon & Schuster, 1998.

———. (Editor). *UFOs and Abductions: Challenging the Borders of Knowledge*. Lawrence, Kansas: University Press of Kansas, 2000.

Jason, Leonard, PhD; Susan R. Torres-Harding, PhD; and Mary Gloria Njoku. "The Face of CFS in the US." *www.cfids.org/special/epi.pdf* (visited 3/21/2012).

Kilstrom, John F. "Hypnosis and Memory." *http://ist-socrates.berkeley.edu/~kihlstrm/hypnosis_L&M2003.htm.* (visited 6/27/2012).

Lamb, Barbara. "Are Human-ET Hybrids In Our Future?". *MUFON 2011International UFO Symposium Proceedings.* p. 98–115.

LeLieuvre, Robert B., PhD; Lester Valez; and Michael Freeman. "Omega 3: Revelation or Revolution—A Comparative Study of Abductees/Experiencers & Community Control Participants". 2010.

Mack, John E., MD. *Abduction: Human Encounters with Aliens.* New York: Charles Scribner's Sons, 1994.

Mack, John, Caroline McLeod, and Barbara Corbisier. "A More Parsimonious Explanation for UFO Abduction." *Psychological Inquiry* 7:2 (1996).

Marden, Kathleen. "Abduction Experiencers' Perceptions of the Alien Agenda." *MUFON 2012 International UFO Symposium Proceedings.* August 2012.

Marden, Kathleen. "Alien Abduction: Fact or Fiction?" *Exposed, Uncovered and Declassified:UFOs & Aliens.* Edited by Michael Pye and Kirsten Dalley. Pompton Plains, New Jersey: New Page Books, 2011.

Marden, Kathleen. "The Conundrum of Alien Abduction." *MUFON 2010 International UFO Symposium Proceedings.* July 2010.

Marden, Kathleen. "Sleep Paralysis or Alien Abduction?" *MUFON UFO Journal.* No. 528 (April 2012) p. 16–23. Also at *www.kathleen-marden.com.*

Neal, Richard. Missing Embryo/Fetus Syndrome: A Preliminary Analysis. *UFO Magazine.* (8/19/1993). *www.ufo-bbs.com/txt3/2554.htm* (visited 9/3/2012).

Project Blue Book Special Report No. 14. Prepared by Battelle Memorial Institute for United States Air Force Project Blue Book, 1955.

Parnell, June O. and R. Leo Sprinkle. "Personality Characteristics of Persons Who Claim UFO Experiences." *Journal of UFO Studies.* 2 (1990). 45–58.

Powers, Susan Marie. "Fantasy Proneness, Amnesia and the UFO Abduction Phenomenon." *Dissociation*. Vol. 5, No. 1 (March 1991) 46–54.

Randle, Kevin D., Russ Estes, and William P. Cone, PhD. *The Abduction Enigma*. New York: Tom Doherty Assoc., 1999.

Redfern, Melvin C., PhD. *Assessment of UFO Witnesses and Experiencers*. E-Book.

Reed Family Abductions. *www.youtube.com/watch?v=UW8T_iGFTyU* (visited 12/1/2012).

Reed Family Second Encounter. *www.youtube.com/watch?v=a_vl0drE-fGs* (visited 12/1/2012).

Reed, Nancy. June 17, 2012 interview with Lorin Cutts. *http://lorin-cutts.com/?p=200* (visited 11/3/2012).

Rodeghier, Goodpastor and Blattenbaur. "Psychosocial Characteristics of Abductees: Results from the CUFOS Abduction Project". *Journal of UFO Studies*. 3 (1991) 59–90.

Rodwell, Mary. "The New Humans," *www.ufocusnz.org.nz/content/The-New-Humans/67.aspx*. (visited 2/26/2012).

Romanek, Stan. *Messages*. Woodbury, Minnesota: Llewellyn Publications, 2009.

———. Stan. *The Orion Regressions*. Hotchkiss, Colorado: Etherean, LLC, 2011.

Saunders, David R. and R. Roger Harkins. *UFOs? Yes!* New York: Signet, 1968.

Schuessler, John E. "UFO Related Human Physiological Effects." A MUFON publication. 1996.

"Sleep Paralysis." January 26, 1999. *www.stanford.edu/~dement/paraly-sis.html*. (visited 3/2010).

"Sleep Paralysis." *www.webmd.com/sleep-disorders/guide/sleep-paraly-sis*. (visited 12/2011).

"Sleep Paralysis and Associated Hypnagogic and Hypnopompic Experiences." *http://watarts.uwaterloo.ca/~acheyne/S_P.html*. (visited 3/15/2012).

Symposium on Unidentified Flying Objects. House Committee on Science and Astronautics. July 29, 1968.

Thavis, John. "Vatican astronomer says if aliens exits, they may not need redemption." Catholic News Service. May 14, 2008. *www.catholicnews.com/data/stories/cns/0802629.htm.* (visited 12/11/2012).

"UFOs and Alien Abductions." The Christian Information Ministries. 6/11/2003. *www.christianinformation.org/article.asp?artID=55* (visited 12/11/2012).

Treurniet, William C. and Paul Hamden. "Extraterrestrial Knowledge of the Energetic Environment." October 2012. *www.treurniet.ca/psi/eenviron.htm.* (visited 12/3/2012).

Vann, Madelyn MPH. "Beyond Exhaustion: Chronic Fatigue Syndrome." *www.everydayhealth.com/chronic-fatigue-syndrome/what-is-chronic-fatigue-syndrome.aspx.* (visited 4/1/2012)

Webb, Walter. "A Dramatic UFO Encounter in the White Mountains, NH." Confidential NICAP Report. October 26, 1961.

"What are Hypnopompic Hallucinations?" *www.wisegeek.com/what-are-hypnopompic-hallucinations.htm.* (visited 1/13/2012).

White, Steve. "Thomas E. Reed Family Abduction." August 1, 2010. *www.ufocasebook.com/2010/reedabduction.html* (visited 10-14-2012).

Wunderground. *www.wunderground.com* (visited 6/24/2012).

Index

About the Authors

Kathleen Marden is a scientific ufologist whose interest in the topic began at a young age. Kathleen is the niece of Betty Hill, who along with her husband, Barney, experienced the first widely publicized alien abduction. She is recognized as the world's leading expert on the Hill's UFO experience.

Kathleen earned her B.A. degree from the University of New Hampshire and participated in graduate studies in education there and at The University of Cincinnati. She was awarded membership to the Alpha Kappa Delta sociology honor society. She began her career as a social worker and later entered into graduate studies in education. During her 15 years as an educator, she innovated, designed, and implemented model educational programs. She also held a supervisory position, coordinating, training, and evaluating education staff. Additionally, she taught adult education classes on UFO and abduction history.

She has engaged in UFO abduction research and investigation for more than 23 years, specializing in the psychology of abduction, hypnosis, and UFO abduction history. Her most recent research project (with Denise Stoner) identified little known commonalities among abduction experiencers.

Kathy is the Mutual UFO Network's Director of Abduction Research. She volunteered as MUFON's Director of Field Investigator Training for

10 years. She was recently named MUFON's 2012 "Researcher of the Year."

She is the author of two books, *Captured! The Betty and Barney Hill UFO Experience* and *Science Was Wrong*, both with nuclear physicist/scientific ufologist Stanton T. Friedman, M.Sc. Her essay "UFO Abductions: Fact or Fiction" appears in *Exposed, Uncovered & Declassified: UFOs and Aliens*. Her articles have been published in the *MUFON UFO Journal*, *Open Minds* magazine, and on several Websites. Kathy has appeared on several television documentaries and more than 100 radio programs in the United States, Canada, and the United Kingdom, and has lectured throughout the United States.

Kathy resides with her family in Florida, and can be contacted at Kmarden@aol.com. Her mailing address is P.O. Box 120172, Clermont, FL 34712. Her website is *www.kathleen-marden.com*.

Denise Stoner is Florida MUFON's Asst. Director of Abduction Studies, a MUFON Field Investigator, and STAR Team member. She heads a Florida research group that is a part of UFO Research of North America, established in 2009, and directed by Butch Witkowski of the UFO Research Center of Pennsylvania. Denise formed the Florida group to increase research and add a scientific approach to new efforts made in Florida in an attempt to come up with more answers regarding the abduction theories already in place. For the past 10 years, Denise has hosted private abductee meetings where attendees come to share their experiences. Her involvement in the UFO field spans more than 21 years.

Additionally, she is Director of the Florida UFO Research Group affiliation of UFORCOP. She also hosts educational forums for the public and a support group for abduction experiencers. Denise has an educational background in business and psychology, and is a certified hypnotist specializing in regressive hypnosis. She has taught classes in stress reduction for more than 12 years for professionals in such fields as medicine and law.

She began her research in hypnosis under Dr. Bob Romack in Denver. They worked together for five years on pain control, smoking cessation, and past-life regression research. Denise also worked as a paranormal investigator in the homes of abductees that felt they had been visited by spirits following abductions. She recorded evidence of the development of psychic abilities in individuals following their experiences with UFOs and ETs, and worked on a team with Dr. Romack studying abductees' abilities to locate missing people and predict future events.

For 12 years, Denise did background investigations for the military on recruits seeking highly classified clearances for work on nuclear submarines. Prior to retirement, Denise moved to a military research facility where she was the training coordinator for several hundred military and civilian employees. Prior to this, Denise spent 8 year with National Park Service in Denver, where she worked on a team who did the planning, design, and construction for the first National Park in Saudi Arabia called the Asir. She also responded to Congressional inquiries and wrote from draft to final form for engineers, scientists, and historians on historic studies, proposals for historic monuments, and trail brochures. She won several monetary awards for her work.

Her retirement from the Federal Government has allowed her to expand her work with UFO research and investigation. Denise has appeared on many radio shows, and speaks yearly at the Daytona Museum of Arts and Science and the Paranormal Investigative Association, Lake Mary History Museum, plus other venues. She has worked as an on-camera expert for documentaries produced in the United Kingdom. She is currently moving forward with some exciting new projects including a television show produced for PBS, hosted by Charlie Carlson, author and TV host of *Weird Florida* that aired in January 2013. She has written two stories for books written by the well-known Sasquatch hunter, author, and university professor, Scott Marlowe. You can contact her at dmstoner1@gmail.com and *www.denisemstoner.com*.